Praise for *Perfect ICT Every Lesson*

Mark Anderson has a well-deserved reputation for his knowledge and enthusiasm for ICT in schools. He has a superb understanding of how ICT can enhance and even transform learning; it's not about innovation for the sake of it or lots of flashy gimmicks. *Perfect ICT Every Lesson* provides an excellent framework for using ICT at a whole-school or classroom level, as well as giving teachers ideas for a range of different strategies and applications. Mark has a gift for making things seem possible. Reading this book will give teachers the confidence to try out some new approaches without worrying that they're not ICT experts. It's an intelligent book, which many teachers will find useful and inspiring.

Tom Sherrington @headguruteacher, Head Teacher, King Edward VI Grammar School, Chelmsford

Perfect ICT Every Lesson seeks to remove the fear some educators have when using ICT to enhance learning. The book dispels the myth that embracing technology in the classroom takes hours of discovery and days of practice before it is exposed to learners. Mark Anderson skilfully discusses techniques and tools whilst maintaining interest in the possibilities that are available to all. The developing pedagogy is outlined to the reader with relevant case studies and examples. There is real craft in the way the learning process is discussed with reference to a tool that should only be used where it is appropriate. Mark successfully informs and relaxes the reader in equal measure. Simple explanation scaffolds the wealth of experience that Mark possesses and it is testament to the author that we are eager to find out more about each suggestion.

I would highly recommend *Perfect ICT Every Lesson* to all educators seeking to continue their own development and enhance learning for their students. This book will sit on top of the reference list when it comes to improving my own methods and I'm thankful it has come along at this stage in my career.

Daniel Edwards @sydedo6, Director of Digital Strategy, Stephen Perse Foundation

In this book, Mark provides us with an exceptionally clear and dynamic vision; full of fantastic strategies, case studies, 'top tips' and suggestions on how to use ICT to transform learning in and out of the classroom. For someone who considers themselves tech-savvy, I still found it packed full of 'Well, I didn't know that' information which had my brain whirring with new possibilities for my own teaching and my school's approach to using technology as a platform for providing deep, creative and memorable learning experiences.

Pete Jones @Pekabelo, Assistant Head Teacher, Director of Learning, Les Quennevais School, Jersey

Mark Anderson's *Perfect ICT Every Lesson* is the most comprehensive, yet accessible, overview of how ICT can be used by all teachers to enhance student learning that I have come across. Quite simply, there is something in it for teachers at every level of responsibility.

What I like most about this book, though, is that it constantly and unerringly sticks to Mark's fundamental principle that it is the learning, not the tech, that is paramount. This is extremely refreshing coming from one of the most technically knowledgeable and proficient educators out there, and I thank him for it.

Fundamentally, the measure of any good educational book is what you learn from it and what you take away from it to implement in your practice. In *Perfect ICT Every Lesson* Mark has handed me the metaphoric 'fish' of some tweaks to make my PowerPoints more PowerFull and to help me use search engines better. More importantly, this book has given me the 'fishing rod' of a far clearer understanding of the SAMR taxonomy, a framework that will help me to think and plan carefully in order to move towards the 'perfect ICT' of the title.

Keven Bartle @kevbartle, Deputy Head Teacher, Canons High School, London

Jam-packed full of accessible and inspirational ideas, the ICT Evangelist has created a companion for every teacher in the land. Mark's real-life shop floor experience instils the reader with the confidence with which to switch on the laptop and start experimenting. Be prepared – this is exciting stuff!

Jamie Portman @JamiePortman, Assistant Head Teacher, Campsmount (a Co-operative Academy), Norton

Mark has written an incredibly useful book, the title of which clearly suggests what it is about; it is not about a 'one off' ICT lesson but about integrating ICT in meaningful ways into everyday lessons to support and extend pupils' learning. It starts with a clear explanation of the SAMR taxonomy, challenging us to think of ways in which we can truly plan for use of technology that will not merely replicate or substitute what could be achieved in a more traditional way; instead, there are illuminating examples of what our pupils can achieve that would have been impossible before. A strength of the book is its plethora of case studies and concrete examples of tasks, with a strong focus on sound pedagogy. Another strength is its plain language and avoidance of unnecessary jargon, making it really teacher-friendly.

Mark addresses current debates such as the use of mobile devices in schools, including a look at the BYOD strategy adopted by some schools. You will learn from this book – I certainly did – a sure sign of a great read.

Hélène Galdin-O'Shea @hgaldinoshea, Head of Media Studies and English teacher

THE PERFECT

ICT LESSON

Every

@ICTEvangelist

Mark Anderson
Edited by Jackie Beere

Independent Thinking Press

First published by
Independent Thinking Press
Crown Buildings, Bancyfelin, Carmarthen, Wales, SA33 5ND, UK
www.independentthinkingpress.com

Independent Thinking Press is an imprint of Crown House Publishing Ltd.

First published 2013.

British Library Cataloguing-in-Publication Data
A catalogue entry for this book is available
from the British Library.

Print ISBN 978-178135103-1
Mobi ISBN 978-178135122-2
ePub ISBN 978-178135123-9

Printed and bound in the UK by
Gomer Press, Llandysul, Ceredigion

For Oscar and Dougie

Contents

Acknowledgements .... *iii*

Foreword .... *v*

Introduction 1

1. Taking ICT from zero to hero 5

2. ICT learning resources for every classroom 23

3. Activities in the ICT suite 45

4. The e-safety framework 61

5. Mobile technology 73

6. Literacy, digital literacy and ICT 95

7. Social media 115

And finally … 129

Bibliography and further reading *131*

Acknowledgements

This book wouldn't exist without the support and inspiration of many people. I would firstly like to acknowledge Jerome Hunt, my first head of department, who revolutionised my teaching from the very start. Secondly, I would like to recognise Sally Thorne, a history teacher from Bristol, who first opened my eyes, via a Twitter conversation, to TeachMeet. Whilst not discussed in this book, TeachMeets have helped me to affect a meteoric rise in my impact as a practitioner. Since attending Sally's TeachMeet, and my subsequent organisation of TeachMeet Clevedon, I have been able to meet and be inspired by hundreds of amazing teachers.

I'd also like to acknowledge the support and vision of Caroline Lenton, Ian Gilbert and Jackie Beere at Crown House Publishing/Independent Thinking Press – without their support and belief in me, I would never have had the opportunity to write this book.

None of this, of course, would have been possible without the support of my colleagues at the amazing Clevedon School. My head teacher, John Wells, and his team – including the mighty Jim Smith – have afforded me opportunities to do things that I don't think many other schools would have let me do, such as develop innovative ways of working, research new pedagogical techniques and try them out in my classroom, and take (measured) risks to bring about improved learning outcomes.

Thanks to those individuals who have offered ideas and encouragement that have inspired my imagination and hunger for educational technological brilliance, in particular Andy Hutt and Tim Rylands.

I must also acknowledge my amazing professional learning network on Twitter of whom there is a cast of thousands. Thank you.

My final acknowledgment must go to my wife (and two amazing boys) without whom this book would never have been written. Countless trips to the zoo and park and many other random destinations, so that Daddy could work on his book, have made this work possible. Without you I would never have had all of these opportunities. Thank you Emma.

Foreword

Teachers have always been in the job of information communication. Now, with the rise of digital media technologies, the means of communicating information is evolving exponentially. How many of us fully use the technology available – not just for the benefit of our pupils, but also for ourselves? How many brilliant lesson ideas have you picked up from Twitter recently, and then delivered using a range of digital media technologies in the classroom?

Teachers who aren't yet using communication devices and social media as learning tools are missing out on some wonderful learning opportunities. But, at home, their pupils are not! They're sharing, joining, blogging, participating, reviewing, filing, photographing, listening, commenting and observing in more amazing ways than ever before. Many children now grow up with smartphones and tablet computers at home, and as soon as they can reach out for them, they begin to play and learn.

Watching 3-year-olds download videos, post photos on their blogs and learn words through iPad games, you start to realise that many teachers are delivering lessons that date from a different era. To fully lead learning today, teachers must be willing to use technology to engage and motivate the young minds which are already immersed in this new world. This requires a mindset open to pushing ourselves out of our comfort zone and getting excited about trying out new technologies in our classrooms.

In this book, Mark Anderson helps teachers find new ways to incorporate ICT into the learning journey – whatever their age, background or familiarity with new technologies. Mark shows how all the key skills your pupils need can be taught using the remarkable new (and not so new) tools of technology and social media.

He is also clear that if we want to be the best teachers we can be, we also have to be learners in the world of ICT. Often, this means sharing expertise by teaching each other but it also involves learning from our pupils. Teachers also need to realise that we are entering a brave new world where CPD will never be the same again. There are huge opportunities to network and communicate using digital media such as Skype, Twitter and blogs linked to TeachMeets and learning forums which are providing a completely new context for professional development.

There has never been a better time to try out new technologies in the classroom and share your successes and challenges with each other in the profession. Mark makes this easy because his ideas are practical and applicable to all lessons and subjects. You will learn so much from just reading this book, but the challenge is to take the ideas and grow them in your classroom. From digital literacy to information searches to e-safety, Mark gives us the practical advice we need to use ICT in a way that suits us and our pupils.

Teachers often long for stability and consolidation rather than for more change or new initiatives. However, the high-speed world of new technology means that this is no longer an option. We all need to react to the world in which our young people live and provide an education that responds to it. If we fail to grasp these new technologies, we risk becoming irrelevant or, even worse, ignored.

Read this book and enjoy experimenting with the ideas it contains in your lessons. At times it may feel risky and scary – but that's learning for you!

Jackie Beere, Tiffield

Introduction

'Noooooo, not the ICT suite! I can't believe I wrote on my performance management targets that I'd use more technology in my lessons!'

The thought of taking pupils from the safe confines of your regular teaching room to the dreaded ICT suite (or 'Computing' as it will be known as from now on) can send even the bravest of teachers running to the hills. The worry that the pupils will know more than you, that you won't be the most knowledgeable person in the room, that there might be a problem and you won't know how to fix it, even those chairs that spin round and offer endless opportunities for misbehaviour ... or, perhaps, like many schools, you now have a bring your own device (BYOD) to school policy or have opted for a 1:1 programme with tablet devices. The trepidation over what pupils will get up to with those devices, and how to use them effectively to secure 'outstanding' use of technology in the classroom, feeds the insecurities of all teachers. It is OK to feel this way though: it is our concern about pupils' success in the classroom that makes us outstanding teachers.

The aim of this book is to take the fears you have and to transform them into confidence – a self-belief that will empower you to use technology enthusiastically, not because you feel you have to, but because you know it will support and enhance the progress your pupils can make. And perhaps, along the way, you will also learn more about making use of devices that are core to 21st century learning.

The advice given in this book will not be a set of hard and fast rules, but practical tips and ideas that you can build upon and add to – to make them your own – so that you have complete ownership of the practice you develop. My philosophy with ICT, and with technology in particular, has always been that I firmly believe that our lives can be made better with it. Think about microwave ovens, mobile phones, television, that amazing thing called Sky+ (when was the last time you had to sit through an advert if you have Sky+?), sat nav, tablet computers and so on. With this philosophy in mind, I always look to technology to help with everything that I do, including in the classroom. Never before has it played such a pivotal role in what we do and how our lives are affected.

The landscape of teaching across the world is changing, as is the way in which children learn.[1] As technology develops and the power of mobile technology, in particular, is being taken up more and more, pupils are embracing this – and it is

---

1   As demonstrated in this useful infographic: http://www.opencolleges.edu.au/infographic/media/21st_century_classroom.jpg/

really helping their progress.[2] Mobile technology has brought about ways of learning that have completely transformed how we can use technology in the classroom.

However, many teachers lack confidence when using technology in the classroom because of concerns that they don't know how to use it properly, so they would rather not. The aim of this book is to empower all teachers, from all sectors and subject areas, to embrace technology as an integral part of their 'outstanding' teaching. You will also learn about the changing world of social media and how savvy use of it can provide you with simply the best continuing professional development you have ever experienced.

This is a world where you can connect with teachers from around the globe, network and get advice to set up amazing experiences for your pupils. Be excited – be very excited …

---

2 For example, there has been a dramatic improvement in results at Essa Academy, in Bolton, where pupils have been using iPod touch devices in the school and results have rocketed: see Chohan (2012).

Chapter 1

Taking ICT from zero to hero

> Secondary schools ... should find ways of making ICT readily accessible to pupils in their classrooms so that it can be used to improve learning in other subjects.
>
> Ofsted, *The Importance of ICT* (2009): 7

If you benchmark the levels of skill, understanding and application of technology by pupils who enter secondary education at age 11 over the last 15 years, their progress has been exponential. This is frequently because of the superb teaching that goes on in many primary schools, but it is also due to other factors:

- Technology has become more affordable and readily available
- Technology has become more intuitive and easy to use
- Technology has become more familiar to pupils at a younger age

- Teachers have become more adept at embedding ICT into the curriculum
- Teachers have become more skilled at using ICT

Pupils are engaged by the use of technology. They are savvy about its use, given that they use technology so much, so it makes sense to leverage their interest, skills and abilities in using technology to enhance learning.

It is already the case that there is no specific subject of ICT; it has become an area of learning which is pervasive throughout every subject. It might mean using spreadsheet software to calculate logical equations in maths, to plot results from an experiment in science, to map tidal ranges in geography, to compare sporting times in PE and so on. Information and communication technologies can be used to enhance the way in which pupils learn right across every phase and every subject.

Historically, of course, the subject of ICT came about as there was a demand from employers for pupils to leave school with a recognised qualification which demonstrated their skill at using particular types of software that would be beneficial in the workplace. Current thinking is starting to shift though. Many pupils now have a large number of these skills by the time they reach the end of their compulsory education, independent of participating in an ICT course. Many people, myself included, believe that whilst pupils do boast many ICT skills, it is important for them to have an opportunity to build on them formally. This will contribute to young people being successful in all areas of the curriculum.

> Teaching is outstanding and, together with a rich and relevant curriculum, contributes to outstanding learning and achievement. ...
>
> Pupils, and particular groups of pupils, have excellent educational experiences at school.
>
> Ofsted, *School Inspection Handbook* (2013): 29

SAMR taxonomy

> ICT was threaded through the whole curriculum of the most outstanding schools. Several of them used cross-curricular planning grids and maps to embed ICT opportunities in all aspects of curriculum planning. In the best curricula there were examples of ICT bringing new learning opportunities to other subjects.
>
> Ofsted, *ICT in Schools 2008–11* (2011): 16

This chapter aims to provide you with a framework which will help you to move from an introductory, or substitutional, use of technology in your lessons to a level that is more transformational. Ruben Puenterdura describes using technology across four different levels – from *substitution* and *augmentation* to *modification* and *redefinition*. He calls it the

SAMR model;[1] where progressing through the various levels takes learners from a basic level of learning in the substitution phase through to a level where learning is transformational at the redefinition level.

> Teachers use well-judged and often imaginative teaching strategies.
>
> Ofsted, *School Inspection Handbook* (2013): 39

What needs to be perfectly clear, however, is that whatever level you are at on this taxonomy for generating learning using technology, it is perfectly OK. Deploying technology in the classroom with pupils is an exceedingly good way of engaging them in learning activities. Young people are familiar with new technologies and devices, even if you aren't, and you will be making small wins (some of which I will discuss below) that will help you find your feet when it comes to using technology in the classroom in a more integrated way.

The SAMR taxonomy enables you to think about how the learning taking place in your classroom could be extended further through your use of technology, thereby making the learning more rich, deep and extensive. For example, if you were developing a geography activity in which you wanted pupils to create a report about the economy of a country, you could ask them to go online and research that area. They

---

1 Dr Ruben Puentedura's blog has information on everything you ever wanted to know about SAMR: http://www.hippasus.com/rrpweblog/

The SAMR model

Transformation	Tech allows for the creation of new tasks, previously inconceivable	Typing but putting online to an expert audience which wouldn't have been previously possible	'Let's create an expert video/interactive book, put it online and share with others or create a video record of our learning and share with others'
		Redefinition
	Tech allows for significant task redesign	Typing but putting online and getting peer review in comments	'Let's make a comic, a digital poster or working collaboratively using Google Docs'
		Modification
Enhancement	Tech acts as a direct substitute, with functional improvement	Typing but enhancing by using an image to represent themes in writing	'Let's highlight some of those words in emotive colours!'
		Augmentation
	Tech acts as a direct tool substitute, with no functional change	Replacing an analogue task, e.g. typing	'Let's type up a story rather than write it in a book!'
		Substitution

could then type up their findings in a word-processed document and hand in the assessment to you when complete.[2] This would be classed as a *substitution* activity. In fact, you could have given your pupils a worksheet and asked them to record this information in their books in the form of a short report. You are basically replacing one way of carrying out the task with another.

At the other end of the spectrum, however, and with the clever use of technology, you could transform the learning substantially – for example, by making online links with industry experts or with another school from that country. This could take the form of pupils talking to each other using a web-based collaborative document – for example, they could post questions and answers via sticky notes on one of the many sticky note sites available. Alternatively, by transforming the learning opportunities even further, they could videoconference with their contacts in a virtual, face-to-face conversation.

Enhancement levels

The bottom two stages of the SAMR model (*substitution* and *augmentation*) represent enhancements of existing ways of working. Tasks can be completed in different ways which are analogue, not digital. You don't really need technology in order to carry out the learning task; the technology is simply

---

2   Encourage students to make use of footers (the space at the bottom of the page) in situations like this to record sources of information, e.g. website addresses.

enhancing the activity with some functional improvement. Examples might include:

- Better presentation
- Spell checking
- Clearer work
- Access to research on the internet
- The ability to correct mistakes easily

Substitution basically means exchanging one thing for another. In the SAMR framework, it involves taking one method of completing a learning activity and replacing it with an equivalent but more technological approach. For example, you could ask pupils to do a handwriting activity in class, the technological equivalent of which would be typing it up on a word processor.

Augmentation is where you take the substitution task and augment or expand on it. Taking our example of typing on a word processor, moving up to augmentation would require introducing a functional improvement. This could be done in a number of ways, such as:

- Adding speech bubbles corresponding to each paragraph and explaining the meaning
- Adding images next to key words to represent what is being demonstrated
- If the writing is an analysis (e.g. business sales), including a graphical representation alongside the written analysis

- Hyperlinking text to information online or including a video to back up your argument
- Colouring the text in a way which represents a mood you are trying to show in the writing or of a character speaking in that paragraph

For example, if you were studying *King Lear* and reflecting upon his madness on the moor, you might like to try:

- Highlighting words in speech bubbles that demonstrate Lear's madness
- Adding images of a storm or of a vexed and troubled person
- Creating a word cloud with adjectives from the play to show the cumulative effect of Shakespeare's word choices
- Linking the text to a recording of Wagner's *Ride of the Valkyries*
- Colouring the relevant text in angry colours such as red, orange or purple

These are all ways in which the work is being augmented beyond the original method of substituting one way of working with another.

Transformation levels

The *modification* and the *redefinition* levels are in a different class to those in the earlier stages. The first two levels don't really change what can already happen in the class without technology. You could, for example, still write out the text in different colours or annotate it in the margins.

These stages include activities that would not have been possible previously without the new technologies. Therefore, technology is actively helping to transform the way in which pupils are learning. Examples might include:

- Videoconferencing
- Narrating a movie they have made
- Creating a screencast to demonstrate knowledge and understanding
- Collaborating on a document with a pupil elsewhere in the world
- Networking with other pupils online using social media (e.g. Twitter)

> There is excellent practice which ensures that all pupils have high levels of literacy appropriate to their age.
>
> Ofsted, *School Inspection Handbook* (2013): 29

To modify our *King Lear* example, we need to look at our task and imagine how it could be completely redesigned using technology. Rather than typing up a piece of work on a word processor, you could ask pupils to set up a blog to record their thoughts and add information similar to that from the augmented activity (e.g. colours and links).

The modification here comes from the opportunity for pupils' work to be opened up to a worldwide audience. The fact that students now have a (potentially) global audience for their blog entries – and know that their work could be seen and commented upon by anyone – means they will spend more time refining their written work. This reinforces their learning and, as a result, their literacy improves substantially.

Case study

Literacy was seen to improve notably at Heathfield Primary School, in Bolton, where the deputy head, David Mitchell, began a journey with the pupils in his school using blogging as a vehicle for improving literacy (and SAT scores).

Literacy had long been a significant issue at the school, particularly with boys. Impressed by a visit he had made to another school, David and his head decided blogging was the way forward for their school. Within seven months, the Year 6 blog had received in excess of 100,000 hits and 1,500 comments.

In the previous year, SAT results saw 9% of pupils achieving Level 5 in writing tests. Following the blogging project, 60% achieved Level 5. Each child, on average, made 6.6 points progress in the 12 months between September 2009 and July 2010. In the next academic year, each child made on average 6.0 points progress. In each of these years, pupils made progress equating to two years progress per child in 12 months.[3]

The work of organisations such as the 100 Word Challenge (100WC), organised by retired head teacher Julia Skinner – which is a weekly creative writing challenge for children under the age of 16 – is a great way to help pupils with their literacy.[4] (The transformations seen at Heathfield Primary School were partly due to engagement with this initiative.) Inspired by weekly prompts, children write a creative piece. This is posted on a class blog and then linked to the 100WC blog. With a massive guaranteed audience for their work, pupils have a far greater motivation for writing well. 100WC participants are also encouraged to comment on the work of others, thus improving literacy through creative writing *and* peer review.

Finally, redefinition involves taking the tasks previously designed by the class teacher and looking at ways in which technology can transform how the learning takes place. The idea here is that the tasks are completed in a way that was not previously conceivable without technology. A good example of task redefinition can be seen in this example from Hotspur Primary School.

---

3   See http://agent4change.net/innovators/982-the-innovators-25-david-mitchell.html/. More information about David Mitchell and the power of blogging as a tool to develop writing can be found at http://deputymitchell.com/about-2/

4   See http://100wc.net/about-100-word-challenge/

Case study

Simon McLoughlin of Hotspur Primary School, in Newcastle upon Tyne, inspired by hearing about how another teacher had connected with a museum in Egypt via Skype, sought ways to include this innovation to help his pupils learn more deeply in class.

The opportunity came when Lord Knight of Weymouth (Jim Knight MP, who was minister of state for schools under the Labour government), left a comment on Twitter about McLoughlin's class blog. Not wanting to miss a chance, Simon contacted Lord Knight, who quickly got back to him with a positive response. He subsequently held a Skype conference with the Year 5 pupils from Simon's class, the purpose of which was to help them learn about the House of Lords and the workings of government.

Transforming learning at the redefinition level of the SAMR framework requires the teacher to think about activities that were previously inconceivable without the use of technology. The example clearly fits into this category. The class were able to speak with someone who was an unmistakable expert in their field and pupils were able to have an exciting experience that had a massive effect on transforming their level of learning and understanding.

---

5 See http://simcloughlin.com/skype-in-my-classroom/

Using the SAMR framework as a planning tool will help you to better examine the learning tasks that you want your pupils to work through. It will also help you to map out and then plan your usage of technology, so the learning in your lessons can become redefined rather than simply enhanced. Letting the pedagogy define how you use the technology, rather than letting the technology drive the curriculum, is a sure-fire way of making sure you don't leave the success of the learning in your classroom to chance. The SAMR framework toolkit below will assist with your planning.

> Ensure that ... where possible, tasks, audiences and purposes [are used] that engage pupils with the world beyond the classroom.
>
> Ofsted, *Moving English Forward* (2012): 7

SAMR framework overview

Level	Definition	Improvement	Stage
Substitution	Substituting an analogue task with a digital one	No functional change	Enhancement
Augmentation	Substituting an analogue task with a digital one with some improvement	Some functional improvement	
Modification	The original task is modified in such a way that learning is transformed	The technology facilitates a significant task redesign which transforms learning	Transformation
Redefinition	The original task is redefined in such a way that learning is significantly transformed in ways that would be inconceivable without technology	Learning is transformed by experiences that would not have previously been possible	

SAMR framework toolkit

Task	How can the learning be enhanced	How can the learning be transformed?	Resources
Example 1: Pupils are researching volcanoes	Pupils research using internet Pupils create a comic with various annotated images showing different layers of a volcano Pupils create a podcast about volcanoes Pupils make a stop motion animation about volcanoes and provide the narration	Pupils blog about volcanoes, getting feedback from other schools Pupils email volcanologists and meteorological experts about volcanoes Pupils videoconference with experts Pupils create their own ebook about volcanoes, narrate it and publish to the world, getting feedback from other schools and experts	Computer or mobile device Internet connection Digital camera Video camera Microphone

Task	How can the learning be enhanced	How can the learning be transformed?	Resources
Example 2: Pupils are learning about the Ming Dynasty	Pupils read an ebook with lots of information and built-in quizzes to test their knowledge on the topic	Pupils create an interactive timeline populated with live links to curated sites of interest	Computer or mobile device Internet connection Digital camera Video camera Microphone
	Pupils research online, while gathering links using a curation tool[6]	Pupils create a comic with the learned information condensed down to act as a learning and revision tool	
	Pupils create a timeline	Pupils comment on each other's blogs about their work	
		The class publish an ebook using their compiled resources (e.g. videos, podcasts, images, poems, artwork) and experts in the field comment on it	

6 There are a number of online tools such as Pinterest, Bitly, Evernote, Scoop.it and Pearltrees which enable you to curate links and online resources into one location for accessing later.

Top tips

- Always ask why you're using digital rather than analogue methods. What does using technology bring to the learning?

- Think about how utilising technology can enhance the learning activity.

- Collaborate with others using new technology to introduce fresh learning opportunities (e.g. blogging).

- Make sure you have high expectations of pupils in terms of their levels of literacy in the work they create.

- Bring the outside world into the classroom using new technology such as Skype.

Chapter 2

ICT learning resources for every classroom

In the good and outstanding schools, there were examples of ICT used creatively and imaginatively in many different subject areas by teachers and pupils to bring subjects alive.

Ofsted, *ICT in Schools 2008–11* (2011): 13

Pupils frequently reported how much they enjoyed using ICT in many different subjects and contexts, at school and at home. A pupil in one school said, 'I like using ICT because I can visit the whole world from my classroom in just one day.'

Ofsted, *ICT in Schools 2008–11* (2011): 12

Teachers and other adults create a positive climate for learning in their lessons and pupils are interested and engaged.

Ofsted, *School Inspection Handbook* (2013): 39

Creating the perfect lesson that incorporates ICT isn't just about the use of ICT in the classroom. Using ICT to prepare resources for lessons is commonplace, but teachers often do not make the best use of the available technology. Sometimes this is due to a lack of knowledge about what tools are available or they simply don't make optimal use of the tools they have.

This chapter aims to provide some clear examples of how various tools can be used in different ways in different subjects. For example, PowerPoint is highly overused but it can be used to make more 'PowerFull' Points. By following the simple steps outlined below, you will make a marked improvement to the quality of learning in your classroom and pupils will be interested and engaged.

What any inspection team (Ofsted or school self-review) wants to know is what is 'typical' of the teaching in a school. This book aims to make sure that your teaching involves using ICT in ways that engage pupils and improve their progress over time.

PowerFull PowerPoints

The PowerPoint presentation is a saviour for many teachers – it is used almost universally, to a greater or lesser extent. It is a long-standing staple in the Microsoft Office suite, so is available to almost all, and is intuitive and user friendly, allowing even the least tech-savvy teacher to produce a presentation. However, it is rarely used powerfully in classrooms.

Slides are frequently overloaded with text and, too often, pupils at the back of the classroom find them difficult to see.

Top Tips

If you want effective presentations in your lessons that show pupils (and any visitors) that you know your stuff, try using the following tips:

- Use contrasting colours between background and font – particularly useful if you have any visually impaired pupils

- Keep font sizes (and fonts) consistent. Don't have lots animations on your slides – simplicity is best

- Keep text information to a minimum – don't try to cram learning outcomes, tasks and hyperlinks all onto one slide. Keep them separate

- Do not read from your presentation. Its purpose is to serve as an inspiration to pupils and as a reminder to you about what you are going to talk about next

- Use key words – three to a slide. Key words alone have far more gravitas than key words combined with extended definitions

- Use images to evoke emotion or to reflect the theme of the lesson

Cont ...

- Use shortcut keys – for example, if you want to grab pupils' attention quickly, simply press 'B' on the keyboard to make the screen go black and press 'B' again to return to normal view
- Move directly to the slide you want by hitting the slide number and pressing the return key

Bringing your walls to life

> The judgement on the quality of teaching must take account of evidence of pupils' learning and progress over time.
>
> Ofsted, *School Inspection Handbook* (2013): 37

One way that you can use ICT to demonstrate the sense of a learning journey in your classroom is through the displays in your room. These set a climate for learning, reflect ongoing work, link to the work that has taken place in your lessons and bring learning to life. Use displays to:

- Recognise pupils' work
- Use pupils' work as part of a learning journey resource
- Kick off starters
- Outline learning outcomes

- Create points for discussion
- Form part of the lesson activity
- Give your room a vibrancy that enhances the climate for learning

Below I outline some examples for different subject areas, as well as ideas to help to make your classroom into an environment that can be linked with technology.

Case study

Every learning space in the school building can be used to engage learners. There are often many 'untapped' learning spaces in schools, such as blank walls. At Clevedon School, in Bristol, plasma screens were installed around the site as information points for pupils. These have been used to optimise learning by the subject leader for art, Kelly Hawkins.

Normally, the plasma screens display a series of different informational slides for pupils, ranging from information about clubs and societies, to sporting fixtures, house competition results and so on. Kelly sees the screens as an opportunity for an added learning space and has created a series of PowerPoint presentation slides. She creates all the slides that are required in one sitting (two per week for every school term). Each slide is branded with a consistent layout: on one slide she includes information about an artist of the week, and on the other slide an art-related word of the week. These slides are then displayed on the various plasma displays around the school.

In this way, Kelly is using ICT to extend the learning for her subject area outside of her classroom. Learning is taking place across the whole of the school landscape and she is reaching pupils who may not even study art.

Word clouds

Taking time to incorporate key words into your lessons has real merit. Key words can help pupils to access higher order vocabulary which, as they learn new words and their meanings, enable them to respond to questions using technical language. This is really important if pupils are going to be capable of conversing in lessons and exams with gravitas, understanding and depth.[1]

Word clouds are a brilliant way of showcasing key words to pupils and they can be used in lots of different ways. A word cloud is a collection of words that have been tiled together, as in the example below. You can make words appear larger within the cloud by repeating them. In this way you can enlarge the key words to reflect their importance.

---

1   See Phil Beadle's *How to Teach* (2010: 93) for some excellent advice on the use of key words.

To create a word cloud you will need to use a word cloud generator. There are many tools available and a quick Google search will throw up some options – my favourite is called Tagxedo.[2] I rate this free tool so highly because it is not only extremely simple to use but because it also has lots of other features that make it supremely suitable for supporting learning. For example, it can generate word clouds automatically from a website address, Twitter feed, input text or the results of a web search. These are especially suitable for learning because it takes the key words from the location you specify and it highlights the key points from that block of text.

By putting a collection of key words into a word cloud you are making your displays look more appealing – and not just by slapping apparently random words up on the wall using your year's supply of Blu-Tack in one go. Word clouds are a fantastic and easy way to bring ICT into your classroom and deliver real learning impact. You can use word clouds to:

■ Showcase the learning outcome for a lesson

■ As part of a starter

---

2 See http://tagxedo.com/

- As a riddle that pupils have to solve
- As clues for what the learning outcome might be for the lesson

Because word cloud generators make frequently used words appear larger within the cloud, this makes them a great learning tool for analysing key themes in any given piece of text. They are useful whether you are analysing a chapter in a book, a website, an individual's tweets or the content of an online debate. The word cloud generated will be of particular use in terms of drawing out important themes for learning.

A superb example of how word clouds can enhance the learning environment is from an English teacher, who took the entire text of *Romeo and Juliet* and turned it into a word cloud in the shape of a heart, like the one below. This was colourfully printed onto A3 paper and displayed on the wall in the classroom, making it a great discussion point and learning tool. Pupils were also given a printed copy so they could make their own notes on it. It brought the classroom walls to life and became an interactive part of the lesson.

The teacher also asked pupils to write their own ideas about the themes shown in the word cloud on a sticky note. Pupils then linked their ideas to the key words in the word cloud on the wall by pinning string from the words in the cloud to their sticky notes. This enabled them to demonstrate the links they had made between the words from *Romeo and Juliet* and the knowledge they had gained in lessons about the play. This activity made the word cloud a central focus in the room, with ideas and resources around it that had been pooled from all of the pupils.

Technical point: In order to reproduce a word cloud on paper, you will need to save a copy from the internet onto your computer as an image and then print it out. You may have to email the image to your reprographics department if you don't have an A3 printer in your department.

QR codes

A QR (quick response) code is a type of image that holds information within it which can be scanned by mobile devices, such as tablet computers or mobile phones. You may have seen them on soft drinks bottles or magazines. A QR code can contain different types of information, including:

- Text (it can hold up to 4,296 alphanumeric characters!)
- Contact information (such as an email address or a phone number)
- Website address
- Link to a YouTube video
- Map reference

They look like this:

You can get apps on mobile devices to scan QR codes. Once the code is scanned, the device will react to the type of information and act appropriately. For example, if you scan the image above, some text will appear saying:

> *QR codes are fantastic bar codes that can hold lots of written information but most powerfully they can link to websites/ resources online.*

QR codes give us a great opportunity to link to lots of different things online, such as:

- Resources that you want pupils to access within your lesson
- The homework you want pupils to complete – pupils simply scan the code to access the text
- A link to any online content that you (or they) have made
- Links to audio explanations or resources you have saved online
- A rubric that you want pupils to follow (e.g. a proofreading code which could be laminated and stuck to desks in your classroom)
- A Thunk,[3] which has been set for homework

QR codes can also be used to bring the walls of your classroom to life in various ways. For example, in art, you usually have the opportunity to display a pupil's art work. However, you don't often get to find out what the pupil was thinking

---

3 A Thunk is 'a beguiling question about everyday things that stops you in your tracks', as defined by Ian Gilbert in his 2007 book, *The Little Book of Thunks*.

when they painted the picture. What was their inspiration? What is their evaluation of the work? Why not add this information underneath the displayed work in a QR code?

If you scan the QR code in the example above, it takes you to a site where you can hear the pupil (well, me!) explaining my reasoning behind my (imaginary) piece of art work.[4] You could add text to the QR code but the activity of getting a student to record themselves is more about sound than writing, plus, with a QR code, the amount of text you can add is limited.

Extending the *Romeo and Juliet* idea further, if you have access to mobile devices in your classroom, you could place various QR codes in a word cloud for pupils to scan. Each code could contain a link which will take pupils to a different resource connected with the play and which require different types of research. For example, they could link to a podcast of a direc-

---

4 See http://soundcloud.com/ictevangelist/art-example/

tor or actor discussing themes in the play, to a video of the play on YouTube or to a website where Leonardo DiCaprio talks about his portrayal of Romeo in the film adaptation of the play.

The uses of QR codes are almost endless – try putting one on:

- Your school prospectus with a link to the school website
- On compliment slips with a link to your school website[5]
- Your classroom door with a link to a video of you welcoming pupils to your class
- Your website with contact details for the school that will automatically be recorded on a parent's phone
- Your pupil planner with links to times tables or other online learning resources
- On the back of reading books with a link to an online audio recording of the book[6]
- Your parent–teacher evening sign-in sheet with a link to an online survey for parents to leave feedback

SOLO stations

As expertly explained in David Didau's *The Perfect Ofsted English Lesson* (2012), SOLO (Structure of Observed Learning Outcome) is an excellent taxonomy which helps to give

---

5 As they do at Highfurlong School, in Blackpool (thanks to Cherryl Drabble).
6 This idea comes from Katie Wilson at Coopers Edge School, in Gloucester, where Key Stage 2 pupils record stories to be listened to by infant pupils.

pupils a language for learning which they can easily understand.[7] SOLO provides pupils with a way to clearly identify what they have learnt within a lesson, how much they have learnt and their level of understanding. You can also use ICT to extend how SOLO is used in lessons to promote independence and as a tool to support electronic SOLO resources.

The taxonomy breaks down the various elements of learning into different phases. For example, think about photosynthesis (see table opposite).

Linked to David Didau's work on this topic – and that of other SOLO luminaries, such as Pam Hook,[8] – Tait Coles of Temple Moor High School, in Leeds, came up with the idea of SOLO stations in his school.[9] SOLO stations are a means of further supporting independent learning within the classroom, which can contribute to creating 'outstanding' Ofsted lessons. We can see this in recent Ofsted publications, such as *Moving English Forward*, which states that the 'criteria for outstanding teaching and learning' includes taking 'every opportunity to encourage pupils to work independently' (Ofsted, 2012: 16–17).

With SOLO stations, resources are organised in the learning environment (which can be virtual[10]) against the different

---

7   For more on SOLO, visit the website of John Biggs: http://www.johnbiggs. com.au/academic/solo-taxonomy/

8   Pam Hook's brilliant resources on SOLO can be found at http://pamhook. com/solo-taxonomy/

9   See http://taitcoles.wordpress.com/2012/05/08/solo-stations/

10 For Tait Coles' extended examination of SOLO Stations using a virtual learning environment (VLE) see http://taitcoles.wordpress.com/2012/09/23/ solo-taxonomy-and-realsmart/

SOLO taxonomy example

Prestructural	Pupils start the lesson with little or no knowledge of the topic. They have a general knowledge that plants need light and water to survive but not much else.
Unistructural	Pupils know (securely) one item about the process of photosynthesis (e.g. 'plants take in carbon dioxide').
Multistructural	Pupils know more than one thing on the topic (e.g. the above, plus 'plants absorb light using the green chlorophyll in their leaves' and 'plants produce oxygen').
Relational	Pupils can take their multistructural knowledge and demonstrate how the elements relate to each other (e.g. pupils take their knowledge related to photosynthesis and create an annotated diagram to demonstrate how it works).
Extended abstract	Pupils take their learning on photosynthesis and apply it to other scenarios (e.g. How does photosynthesis relate to food chains? What is its effect on the carbon cycle? Can photosynthesis be used to combat global warming?).

levels of the taxonomy. The resources are pitched in ways that allow pupils with different levels of understanding to learn and make progress to the next level. Based upon their prior knowledge, pupils choose which level they are at in the taxonomy. They then move to that level and access the resources available. However, as we know, pupils are not always the best judges of their level of understanding, so it is positively encouraged that they are honest about whether they have enough knowledge, skill and understanding at their chosen level to complete the task. If necessary, they can go back a level (e.g. from relational back to multistructural, to access those resources, before they make the jump back up to the relational level).

The SOLO taxonomy employs five symbols attached to each level of understanding, skill and mastery:[11]

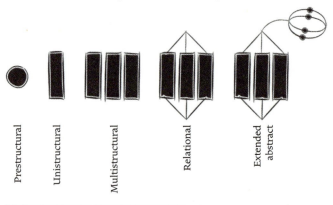

Prestructural

Unistructural

Multistructural

Relational

Extended abstract

11 Biggs, John B. and Collis, Kevin F. (1982). *Evaluating the Quality of Learning: The SOLO Taxonomy* (Educational Psychology Series). New York: Academic Press.

In Tait Coles' original example, the SOLO stations resources were placed around the room and pupils accessed analogue resources within the class. Alternatively, you could create virtual SOLO stations around the room. Use the SOLO taxonomy symbols to denote the different SOLO levels, with QR codes alongside them to link to the success criteria for each station and other codes which link to resources to support the learning at each of the stages.[12] So long as the resource is stored online, the QR code could link to anything, such as:

▨ YouTube clips

▨ A collaborative online document (e.g. Google Drive)

▨ A downloadable PDF resource

▨ A podcast

▨ A poster

Even better, leave the framework on the wall and let the pupils create their own resources, which will demonstrate their unistructural, multistructural, relational and extended abstract understanding. You will then have a set of resources, including all the QR codes, which pupils can photograph and refer to when revising the topics for examinations.

---

12 You could also have the QR codes printed alongside the text – this may in fact make the success criteria more explicit for the pupils.

Flipping your classroom

The idea of 'flipping' (or reversing) your classroom refers to the way in which pupils work in your lessons and at home – it is a style of 'blended learning'.[13] Rather than pupils completing independent work in lessons and homework on classroom activities at home, they instead complete (technologically guided) learning activities at home, making use of materials you have prepared earlier. Often this is done through the use of screencasts (a short video where a topic or skill is explained or demonstrated – see Chapter 5 for more on this) or other resources that might be placed on your school's virtual learning environment (VLE),[14] a YouTube channel or other learning platform. When pupils complete work in their own time, you are better able to use your time in class to act as a facilitator to deal with any problems with learning that have arisen whilst pupils were working on tasks outside of class.

When setting blended learning tasks, be mindful that not every family has access to technology at home, so check there are opportunities in your school for pupils to access technology (e.g. lunchtime clubs or after-school sessions).

---

13 Blended learning is a model which combines face-to-face teaching with technology-mediated activities.

14 There are lots of VLEs available. These are learning platforms where teachers and learners can access, submit, assess and share work across different classes within a whole school.

Further information: The term 'flipped classroom' came about following an article by Daniel Pink (2010), in which he wrote about how edtech guru Karl Fisch was giving pupils screencasts for them to work on from home. In the article, Pink called this the 'Fisch flip' and thus the name was born. Karl Fisch credits his inspiration to Aaron Sams[15] and Jon Bergman.[16] Flipped learning has been brought even further into the consciousness of the public by the work of Salman Khan, whose Khan Academy has tens of thousands of pupils and teachers using his videos every week.[17]

So how do you flip your classroom? In the first instance, you can always refer pupils to the plethora of existing examples, such as the ones found in the Khan Academy, which includes hundreds of videos on many different topics covering a massive curriculum base. These types of screencast will certainly be a good place of reference for you and your pupils. They will also give you a basic idea about the level of detail and proficiency you might want to achieve with any resources you wish to produce. Using existing materials is a positive way of supporting pupils with their learning; however, it is always recommended that you create your own so that you are per-

15 See http://chemicalsams.blogspot.co.uk/2011/10/there-is-no-such-thing-as-flipped-class.html/
16 See http://flipped-learning.com/
17 Watch a TED Talk by Khan at http://www.ted.com/talks/salman_khan_let_s_use_video_to_reinvent_education.html/ or visit http://www.khanacademy.org/

sonalising the learning in the context of your pupils in your classes.

There are lots of ways to create resources to support a flipped classroom:

■ Create a screencast. These usually involve a series of slides generated from a computer screen output with accompanying audio narration, but they can also include your face if you want them to! There are various free and paid versions of software that allow you to do this. The industry standard 'paid for' software is Camtasia Studio by Techsmith,[18] which has been the market leader for some time. However, there are free versions such as Jing[19] and Screencast-O-Matic[20] which can give a very similar result.

■ On-screen recordings. Many tablets, such as the iPad, have lots of 'virtual whiteboard' apps which allow the user to talk whilst recording and showing learning materials.[21] One of the big bonuses with working in this way is that tablets allow you to annotate live on screen as you are working through your delivery.

---

18 See http://www.techsmith.com/Camtasia/
19 See http://www.techsmith.com/jing.html/
20 See http://www.screencast-o-matic.com/
21 These are examined in more detail in Chapter 5 with apps such as Explain Everything.

Top tips

- Consider the use of word clouds, QR codes and SOLO stations in your classroom.

- Take time to ensure that your classroom wall displays reflect the learning taking place.

- Make your PowerPoint presentations PowerFull by not cluttering your slides with too much information.

- Think outside the classroom by considering how you can use different areas of your school environment to enhance learning.

- Flip your classroom. A great independent learning opportunity is to ask pupils to utilise technology to create their own learning episodes to demonstrate their knowledge, understanding and skill. These can then be shared across the class and peer reviewed.

Chapter 3

Activities in the ICT suite

Ofsted does not have a preferred style of teaching. Inspectors will simply judge teaching on whether children are engaged, focussed, learning and making progress.

Sir Michael Wilshaw (2012)

For many years, primary and secondary schools in the UK have had an area in the building where whole classes can use desktop workstations, most commonly PCs running Microsoft Windows. Schools are now moving away from this model as it tends to compartmentalise ICT as a subject, when ICT really needs to pervade every aspect of school life. The idea that there are rooms where you go 'to do IT' doesn't help anyone to see how technology can support learning across the whole curriculum. It also means that technology is rooted to one physical location. This is problematic when what you want is for your pupils to be mobile or you only want them to have brief access to technology in your lesson. More schools are beginning to embrace mobile learning opportunities through 1:1 tablet schemes and BYOD models (which will be discussed in Chapter 5).

However, for the time being, this is not the case for most schools. So, how do we make best use of the ICT suite?

1. Familiarise yourself with the room. ICT suites are almost always laid out rigidly, so it isn't easy to facilitate group work. Plan your seating accordingly.

2. Prepare sequences of lessons. It is unlikely that you will want to use the ICT suite for just one lesson, so plan for this.

3. Add in contingency time – things will go wrong from time to time. It is easier to give up a booked room than it is to get it back from a colleague who has jumped in straight after your sequence of lessons.

4. Set up clear structures and routines for saving and sharing work (and build in time to facilitate this). You want pupils to be able to quickly access and share their work with you and others.

5. Test out any applications, particularly web applications, you want to use at school before your lesson takes place. Just because the fantastic resource you've found from home is amazing, it doesn't necessarily mean that it will work in your school. Use a pupil account to do this because, in many schools, teachers often have a

different access level to that of pupils; so whilst it might work for you, it might not for them.

6. ICT suites usually have network tools on the teacher machines. If your school has them, familiarise yourself with these before the lesson – they often have fantastic features to support learning and behaviour for learning, such as:

■ Blanking screens

■ Polling

■ Only allowing pupils access to the sites you select

■ Displaying a pupil screen to all screens

■ Displaying a teacher's screen to all screens

Top tips

If you have been working with the class prior to going to the ICT suite, and have been using a wall display as the basis for thinking in class, take a photo of the display and include it in your already PowerFull PowerPoint. This will act as a memory jogger for pupils in the lesson.

Blogging

> [T]eachers and learners now live in a world where communication and knowledge are routinely digital, ubiquitous and highly interactive ... the processes of learning and teaching can, and must, take advantage of what digital technologies offer.
>
> Digital Classroom Teaching Task
> and Finish Group (2012): 4

Tapping into this 'digital, ubiquitous and highly interactive' world can be done through blogging. A blog (or web log to give it its full title) is a collection of posts or articles that are written and can be commented upon. So, how do you set one up? There are a number of providers that give excellent opportunities for class blogs such as Edublogs and Kidblog. To start one you simply need to visit their site, give your blog a name and away you go. The two mentioned here are free and offer good levels of protection through passwords. Most allow you to post an article simply by sending an email. There is lots of online help, too, from the providers which will support you as you develop your blog.

E-safety (which will be covered in more detail in Chapter 4) should always be at the forefront of your mind when asking pupils to complete work online. Some general rules should always apply:

■ Only use pupils' first names

■ Do not post pictures of pupils online, particularly where parental permission has not been given – best practice is to blur out children's faces[1]

■ Moderate blog articles and comments – this means, as class teacher, that you check blog articles and comments before they go online

The use of blogging as a learning tool enables activities that provide stimulus, collaboration, rapid access to resources and pupil creativity. Blogs can be used to:

■ Submit work electronically

■ Record learning and progress from a lesson

■ Reflect upon learning

■ Write creatively

■ Curate resources found from other places

■ Share ongoing classwork with parents

Blogging in the primary setting is very popular. Many classes have their own blogs and make great use of initiatives such as QuadBlogging.[2] This scheme involves working with three

---

1   You can do this using a free tool available at http://www.picmonkey.com/
2   See http://quadblogging.net/

other schools to guarantee an audience for a class blog and it incorporates a feedback regime across all four schools. Ofsted praised Haworth Primary School in their 2012 Ofsted report saying:

> Regular blogging provides pupils with speedy feedback from their peers and from a global audience about their thoughts and work. ...
>
> The school's 'linking school project' maintains close links with a school in inner-city Bradford so pupils acquire meaningful understanding of diversity. This is magnified through the school's 'quadblogging' and its link with Jamaica. ...
>
> Pupils know very well how to keep themselves safe. They are clear about how important it is to use the internet carefully as well as other new technologies.
>
> Ofsted, *Haworth Primary School: Inspection Report No. 377559* (2012): 6

Blogging across different subject areas in secondary settings is also becoming increasingly popular. If you have the technology available, you can make blogging work for you in whatever setting you are in.

Asking pupils to submit their work electronically has some huge benefits:

- There is no need for you or your students to carry around loads of books
- Parents can easily view their children's work[3]
- It allows easy tracking of comments
- It is inexpensive
- It is an effective, proven tool to support and improve learning

> Consistently high quality marking and constructive feedback from teachers ensure that pupils make rapid gains.
>
> Ofsted, *School Inspection Handbook* (2013): 39

Blogging also provides an excellent platform for the sharing and discussion of feedback, both from teachers and peers. It is a brilliant way for pupils to develop resilience, to be inspired by the real-life audience that blogging to the world can bring and to improve their work through the critique and feedback of others. As John Hattie (2012) observes, 'Feedback is among the most common features of successful teaching

---

3   Many schools run sessions which train parents in how to access their child's school blog. Kidblog and Edublogs allow you to password protect blogs too, so only parents and school members can view them.

and learning'. He adds that the aim is to provide feedback that is:

> ▨ Just in time.
>
> ▨ Just for me.
>
> ▨ Just for where I am in my learning process.
>
> ▨ Just what I need to help me move forward.
>
> Hattie (2012)

The fact that blogs support comments on articles makes them exceedingly powerful indeed. Teachers who wish to activate commenting on blogs created by pupils can do this easily using the built-in commenting tools that appear on all of the blogging platforms. Some schools and departments have chosen to replace exercise books entirely with an online version in the form of a blog.

Case study

Chris Waugh of the London Nautical School has transformed his English department by making every pupil's exercise book into a class blog called 'Edutronic'.[4] Everything the pupils do is recorded here. According to Chris, 'Edutronic is a comprehensive, custom-designed,

---

4   See http://www.edutronic.net/

pupil blogging platform for English classes. There is a blog for each class with a lesson stream that tracks and compiles the daily traffic of the classroom.' Year plans, samples of excellent pupil work, moderated exemplars, lesson sequences, videos of pupils speaking and teaching practice also appear on the site.

As all of the evidence is online, the blog makes it clear how much progress has been made over time. Pupils post their work, Waugh gives them feedback and the pupils improve and refine their work. With learning and progress being so visible, fantastic opportunities open up for pupils to develop – with technology being used to achieve this.

Pupils are getting prompt, regular feedback from teachers, which ties in with John Hattie's requirements. As a result, pupils are able to make rapid gains since the 'marking and constructive feedback from teachers contributes to pupils' learning' (Ofsted, 2013: 18). This is great for the pupils and their progress, and certainly something that Ofsted would be very happy to see.

Creating a blog for your pupils will clearly take time. However, once it has been set up, the rewards of having all of this information readily available for pupils, parents and their global audience has a big impact. Since implementing Edutronic, the London Nautical School has seen a massive 14% rise in A*-C grades in their English language papers, which, as Waugh asserts, is a clear 'indication that we're on the right track with our new initiatives'.[5]

> Secondary schools and primary schools should ... improve the use of assessment of pupils' progress in ICT, ensuring that pupils know how well they are doing and what they should do to move on to the next level.
>
> Ofsted, *ICT in Schools 2008–11* (2011): 7–8

Collaboration

Historically, the internet has been a great place for researching and gathering ideas – a site for the consumption of media. This still goes on to this day. However, in the past decade, a more cumulative version of the internet has emerged which has collaboration at its heart. Darcy DiNucci came up with the term Web 2.0 in 1999, but it became more generally known after the O'Reilly Media Web 2.0 conference at which Tim O'Reilly (2005) suggested there was a new type of interactive web environment.

Historically, websites had contained static content: resources could be accessed but there were no online applications with which users could interact. The development of blogs, wikis, video sharing, web applications and more brought about a

---

5   See http://www.edutronic.net/2012/08/23/gcse-success/

massive shift in how everyone, including teachers and learners, could interact with the online world.

One of the biggest players in this field has been Google. They have created lots of ways in which we can interact and work collaboratively using technology anywhere, on any device, at any time. Their online application Google Drive (formerly Google Docs) has many features which allow multiple users to work on documents at the same time. In writing this book, similar features have been used between author and editor to track changes and collaborate on different ideas. You, too, can use these ideas with pupils in your lessons. Here are some examples:

- Writing. With Google's Word Processor and the 'Review' tool in Microsoft Word, you can support collaborative working by allowing online sharing of documents between different pupil users (see more on this in Chapter 6). When working in groups, pupils can collaborate on one document and make comments using the inline commenting options. In the context of peer assessment, pupils can comment on work 'live' and feed ideas into the main piece of writing.

- Presentation. Using Google's presentation tool, pupils can work collaboratively on a presentation at the same time and use the inline commenting tools.

- Google Drive. All of the tools held within the Google Drive application allow collaboration. Furthermore, as a cloud-based service, it allows you to store files online which can then, in turn, be shared with others – either for viewing or for collaborating on together. Cloud computing offers a number of significant benefits for teachers and pupils, who can work together on various documents on virtually any platform, mobile or desktop, and feed this into team work.

Case study

Mat Pullen, of the City Academy, Bristol,[6] has been using the commenting facility in Google Drive to great effect on iPads in his BTEC PE lessons. He has created a system where department documents are stored online on Google Drive, which all members of his team can access to update and comment on. He has also shared these files with his pupils across various classes who can also read and copy them.

Teachers have access to students' work files, so when a pupil completes an assignment, teachers (and pupils) can comment on these pieces of work. Teachers are able to respond to pupils' work quickly and efficiently on their iPads when on the move – whether out on the pitch, in the gym or in the classroom. The benefit for the pupils is that they can immediately see what progress they have made, note any improvements they still need to make

---

6   Take a look at Mat Pullen's blog: http://matpullen.com/

and whether or not they have passed specific sections of their BTEC assessments.

The system has proven to be very popular and it is easy to understand why: the departmental team has become more efficient, assessment has become easier, and progress and learning are more visible. If, as John Hattie says, pupils' understanding of their achievement must be 'enhanced to the degree that pupils develop self-strategies: to seek and receive feedback to verify rather than enhance their sense of achievement efficacy' (Hattie, 1999), then this strategy does that with aplomb.

There are lots of ways that you can make good use of the ICT suite to explore, develop and enhance the learning process. The opportunities outlined in this chapter are certainly not exhaustive but, by using these ideas and coupling them with your own imagination and thinking linked to the SAMR framework in Chapter 1, you will be able to ensure that any application can be purposeful and transformational – and isn't constrained by a specific room!

Top tips

- Plan your time effectively – it's not your regular classroom so familiarise yourself with the tools on offer in the room.
- Book sequences of lessons that link directly to classroom work.
- Use tools that facilitate peer review and collaboration.
- Extend work outside the classroom by utilising tools such as class blogging.
- Take presentation seriously – you do it when pupils write in their textbooks, so make sure work is presented consistently and clearly when using technology too.
- Have records of pupil achievement recorded in a spreadsheet to easily and clearly demonstrate progress over time.
- Make sure pupils (and you) have a structure for saving work – you don't want pupils to come to the next lesson not being able to find the work they created last lesson.
- Use the network tools that are likely to be in the room to support behaviour for learning.
- Most desktop monitors have glass-fronted screens (check first!), so if you are working with a pupil on

a one-to-one basis, use a whiteboard marker to write on the monitor if it helps – it will rub right off!

Chapter 4

The e-safety framework

> The breadth of issues classified within e-safety is considerable.
>
> Ofsted, *Inspecting E-safety* (2012): 4

This book is not about e-safety but, certainly, the use of ICT in schools has massive implications when it comes to security. With recent directives from Ofsted regarding e-safety and the implications it has on whole-school inspection, it is clear that this needs to be addressed.

This chapter goes into some depth about how leadership teams might like to proceed in order to ensure compliance with Ofsted requirements. Within Ofsted's Section 5 briefing papers for use during inspections, published in September 2012, was a paper called *Inspecting E-Safety*,[1] in which they systematically break down and give clear guidance on what

---

1   Available at: http://www.ofsted.gov.uk/resources/briefings-and-information-for-use-during-inspections-of-maintained-schools-and-academies-september-2/

outstanding practice should look like. Ofsted clearly link it to seven key areas: (1) whole-school consistent approach, (2) robust and integrated reporting routines, (3) staff, (4) policies, (5), education, (6) infrastructure and (7) monitoring and evaluation.

In practice this will involve schools adopting safe and responsible practices in relation to all technologies in order to protect children from inappropriate content, grooming, cyber-bullying, identity theft, privacy and teachers being mindful of their own use of technology, both inside and outside of school.

Whole-school consistent approach

Ofsted make it clear that e-safety should be high on the agenda for everyone in the school if pupils are to be safe whilst online. They state that the key features of a whole-school consistent approach should include:

> ▨ All teaching and non-teaching staff can recognise and are aware of e-safety issues.
>
> ▨ High quality leadership and management make e-safety a priority across all areas of the school (the school may also have achieved a recognised standard, for example the e-Safety Mark).

> ■ A high priority [is] given to training in e-safety, extending expertise widely and building internal capacity.
>
> ■ The contribution of pupils, parents and the wider school community is valued and integrated.
>
> Ofsted, *Inspecting E-Safety* (2012): 7

This means ensuring that staff are given opportunities to learn about e-safety, and receive training on protecting their professional identity and how e-safety relates to their teaching practice. Best practice would mean that training happens on a regular basis and that effective e-safety pervades all electronic work. Consider it as risk assessment for using online tools. Always think carefully about how students are going to work whilst online and what e-safety implications might arise – then mitigate against any potential problems.

Robust and integrated reporting routines

The key features Ofsted recognise in relation to reporting routines are that:

■ School-based online reporting processes ... are clearly understood by the whole school, allowing the pupils to report issues to nominated staff, for example SHARP.[2]

■ Report Abuse buttons, for example CEOP.[3]

Ofsted, *Inspecting E-Safety* (2012): 7

Recommended best practice is to have the CEOP report abuse button on the school's home page, with a link to the CEOP website. In addition to this there should be clear guidance on how students report issues relating to e-safety and cyber-bullying. The cyber mentors scheme run by BeatBullying is a good place to look for support, training and guidance.[4]

2　The School Help Advice Reporting Page (or SHARP) is a system which enables schools to activate a series of reporting options and web pages which can be accessed from mobile phones and other devices. Visit http://www. thesharpsystem.com/ for more information.

3　The Child Exploitation and Online Protection Centre (CEOP) is affiliated to the Serious Organised Crime Agency and aims to eradicate the sexual abuse of children. Visit http://ceop.police.uk/ for more information.

4　Visit http://www.beatbullying.org/

Chapter 4

Staff

Ofsted recommend the following with regard to staff training:

- All teaching and non-teaching staff receive regular and up-to-date training.
- At least one staff member has accredited training, for example CEOP, EPICT.[5]

Ofsted, *Inspecting E-Safety* (2012): 7

It is advised that staff also receive training on protecting their professional identity. Many teachers using social media are ill-prepared for the ramifications of their online activities in their working lives.[6] This is not to advocate poor choices in teachers' free time, but it is about making sure that professionals know that how they conduct themselves when online is very important.

---

5 The European Pedagogical ICT (EPICT) Licence is a Europe-wide training standard which includes e-safety.

6 One example of how things can go wrong involved staff from a primary school who in 2011 unwisely published photos of their drunken night out on Facebook. Their profiles were not set to private and the images could be viewed by anyone. The story later made it into the national press: http://www.dailymail.co.uk/news/article-1389292/Disgrace-drinking-pole-dancing-primary-school-teachers-published-pictures-Facebook.html/

Policies

Ofsted recognise that outstanding practice occurs where:

▓ Rigorous e-safety policies and procedures are in place, written in plain English, contributed to by the whole school, updated regularly and ratified by governors.

▓ The e-safety policy should be integrated with other relevant policies such as behaviour, safeguarding and anti-bullying.

▓ The e-safety policy should incorporate an Acceptable Usage Policy that is signed by pupils and/or parents as well as all staff and respected by all.

Ofsted, *Inspecting E-Safety* (2012): 7–8

In my experience, involving all stakeholders in the process of creating e-safety policies is key for engaging participation and buy-in and for ensuring policies are adhered to by all. It is critical to involve parents in training sessions and provide opportunities for them to learn about e-safety too. Whole community involvement is a brilliant way to do this – involving primary and secondary schools, parents and teachers in the discussion. Working together and building a culture of e-safety in a community helps everyone to be stronger. Many organisations can offer help with this process – for example,

Vodafone provides an excellent free service for parents including a magazine called *Digital Parenting*.[7]

Education

Ofsted assert that outstanding practice in schools includes:

▓ A progressive curriculum that is flexible, relevant and engages pupils' interest; that is used to promote e-safety through teaching pupils how to stay safe, how to protect themselves from harm and how to take responsibility for their own and others' safety.

▓ Positive sanctions are used to reward positive and responsible use.

▓ Peer mentoring programmes.

Ofsted, *Inspecting E-Safety* (2012): 8

---

7   Visit http://www.vodafone.com/content/parents.html for more information.

Infrastructure, monitoring and evaluation

Ofsted also recognise the importance of:

▨ Recognised internet service provider or RBC [regional broadband consortia] together with age related filtering that is actively monitored.

▨ Risk assessment taken seriously and used to good effect in promoting e-safety.

▨ Using data effectively to assess the impact of e-safety practice and how this informs strategy.

Ofsted, *Inspecting E-Safety* (2012): 8

How to develop outstanding e-safety practices

Incorporating the ideas from the seven key areas outlined above is crucial to ensuring that your school is doing all it can to protect the e-safety of pupils. There are a number of ways to achieve this, but a steering group made up of key individuals who feed through to influence whole-school policy and monitoring is a good place to start. A team including the following people is a recommended minimum: head teacher, child protection officer, link governor (parent), head of ICT and head of technical team.

A good place to find out exactly where your school is at in terms of online safety coverage is to use the South West Grid for Learning's 360° free e-safety self-review tool.[8] It is a great way to honestly gauge and then direct movement towards outstanding practice and procedure in your school. The tool outlines key areas of responsibility, which you can combine with the other recommendations in this chapter. Once you have completed the 360° review, you will be provided with a plan of any necessary improvements required to bring your school up to standard – an excellent roadmap to ensuring excellent practice.

The self-review tool covers important areas organised under four distinct headings.

1. Education
   - Children and young people
   - Community – extended schools
   - Governors
   - Parents and carers
   - Staff

2. Infrastructure
   - Passwords
   - Services

3. Policy and leadership
   - Communications and communications technologies
   - Policies
   - Responsibilities

---

8 Visit http://www.360safe.org.uk/ for more information.

4. Standards and inspection

   ▓ Monitoring

If you think your school has scored highly, then you can apply (and pay) for the E-Safety Mark, which provides recognition of the outstanding work that goes on in schools in relation to e-safety. The process of compiling the evidence for accreditation – ensuring that acceptable use policies and agreements, safeguarding and other relevant documentation are in place – will also mean you are fully prepared for any questions Ofsted may ask relating to whole school e-safety when they arrive.

Acceptable use policies and digital citizenship

An acceptable use policy (AUP) is a document which states what uses of new and emerging technologies are acceptable in your school and any sanctions for misuse. For a school to deliver a successful, modern curriculum which embraces the use of technology and computing, and still manage its e-safety requirements, a fine balance must be struck. It is crucial to have an AUP in place which will adequately protect pupils, staff and the school. Overbearing and limiting policies will produce scenarios in which pupils miss out on essential learning opportunities. However, lack of monitoring and management can lead to unpleasant situations. It is important to produce an AUP which allows exciting and vibrant modern technologies to be used, whilst being mindful of some of the less desirable elements of the World Wide Web and some of the people who frequent it.

When it comes to creating e-safety policies, best practice is to involve all stakeholders. This means including parents, pupils, staff, senior leadership and governors. The e-safety steering group (discussed above) should be a representative body. In many schools, a copy of the AUP must be signed before pupils are allowed to make use of the school's ICT and Wi-Fi facilities. This is not particularly draconian; it is common practice to register for free Wi-Fi in cafes and fast-food outlets where certain terms and conditions apply. It is right that these rules are in place to protect all concerned.

A good AUP should cover at least the following areas:

- Network access
- Internet access
- Wi-Fi access
- Security of data
- Respecting yourself and others
- Protecting yourself and others
- Protecting and respecting intellectual property

In summary, all teaching and non-teaching staff should be aware and able to recognise e-safety issues, with the senior leadership team making this a high priority. The school should have clear reporting processes and ensure that excellent risk assessment mechanisms are in place. High priority should be given to the continual training of all staff, including the wider school community.

Top tips

- Make sure you are aware of the contents of Ofsted's *Inspecting E-Safety* briefing sheet.

- Get together a team of stakeholders (ideally including those mentioned above).

- Complete the 360° e-safety tool and action any discrepancies.

- Create an AUP in line with best practice.

- Develop rigorous, plain English policies and procedures, which are integrated with other relevant policies and developed in conjunction with all stakeholders.

- Support stakeholders in becoming aware of e-safety and how to safeguard it.

- Ensure e-safety is visible – through posters, lessons, plans and actions.

- Use a recognised internet service provider (ISP) which deploys age-related filtering.

Chapter 5

Mobile technology

With their tactile interface, touchscreen devices are very appealing and many students are adept at using them. Capitalising on their interest in these devices is a great way to engage students in learning. In this chapter we will examine how to capitalise on the opportunities brought about by mobile learning and to make sure that the learning in a mobile-rich environment remains deep and purposeful.

The educational experiences of individuals now in their thirties, forties and older, compared with those delivered in schools today, are worlds apart. Certainly in the subject area of ICT and computing, the topics pupils learn about in lessons were not even invented 15 or 20 years ago. This could explain, to a large extent, why many teachers find using technology so demanding.

Marc Prensky (2001) first coined the terms 'digital natives' and 'digital immigrants'. More than a decade on, what he says is still correct, to a certain extent. Pupils now arrive at school increasingly better equipped with abilities and competencies in using technology. This is also true of many new teachers – there has been a definite increase in the confidence of teachers in the use of ICT in their classrooms over the past decade or so.

That said, technology has come on in leaps and bounds over recent years. Much of what was science fiction 20 years ago is now science fact. There is more processing power in the pocket of your average teenager than was used on the 1969 mission to the moon. In computing, there is a phenomenon called Moore's Law, which states that the number of transistors on integrated circuits doubles approximately every two years. This law has parallels in all aspects of technology – for example, processing speed, memory capacity and pixels in digital cameras are all increasing at an exponential rate.

Due to these huge technological advances, pupils in schools now have access to learning opportunities which didn't exist even as recently as five years ago. Mary Meeker and colleagues (of Morgan Stanley) said in their 2012 *Internet Trends* report that by 2014 the number of mobile internet users would exceed the number of desktop internet users.[1]

The introduction of the iPad a few months later had a massive impact on their predictions. We are seeing things re-imagined before our very eyes. The ways in which young people are interacting with technology today, and will go on to interact and learn with in the future, has changed radically

---

1   Mary Meeker, Scott Devitt, and Liang Wu (2012), *Internet Trends*, Slide 8.
    Available at: http://www.scribd.com/document_downloads/29850507?extension
    =pdf&from=embed&source=embed/

and we are at a turning point in our technological development.

After 224 years, 2012 saw the *Encyclopaedia Britannica* go out of print. Microsoft shut down their Encarta service in 2009 and now Wikipedia has 470 million monthly unique visitors. The way in which pupils are going to learn in the classroom is changing and will continue to do so as more advancements are made (such as through the ongoing development of Google Glass).

> In two schools, teachers were trialling the use of tablet PCs to photograph work during lessons, in an enterprising initiative to assess and record progress. One school had purchased 30 handheld games consoles, specifically to improve speed and accuracy in mental arithmetic. The challenge generated by these arithmetic games excited the pupils and resulted in high levels of concentration.
>
> Ofsted, *ICT in Schools 2008–11* (2011): 15

When it comes to mobile learning, there are two main models being adopted by schools and teachers: (1) banning it and sticking our heads in the sand, and (2) embracing it with schemes such as BYOD and 1:1.

Mobile learning: ban it

If we are going to give our pupils excellent educational experiences in school – given all the information available on how young people are going to work in the future and how they are interacting with it now – we must look to mobile technologies. If, as a school, you are not going to embrace new technology, and in particular mobile technology, then you are going against a tsunami of evidence which shows that the rest of the world is adopting this route and, whether you like it or not, your pupils will be too. Whether it is in how they work at home, revise or access information in-between lessons, it is going to happen and already is happening. Embrace it.

Fraser Speirs, the man responsible for introducing the first 1:1 iPad scheme for schools in the world, spoke recently at an Apple conference.[2] He said that he frequently thinks about his child and her future – his daughter is currently 3. When she reaches the age of 22, following school and university, he wonders whether technology is more or less likely to be involved in her life, working or otherwise. The answer is obvious. So, as professionals, we should be making sure we give our pupils the best possible opportunities to use technology to support learning, and be working to provide a rich and relevant curriculum which contributes to outstanding learning and achievement.

---

2   Apple Leadership Summit, Cadbury House, Bristol, November 2012.

All evidence indicates a point in time when all pupils will be embracing learning using mobile technology. In his report, *Education and the Impact of Mobiles and Mobility*, John Traxler writes how 'interacting with mobile technologies is different and is difficult to ignore as they are woven into all times and places of users' and learners' lives' (2009: 3).

The Nesta report *Decoding Learning* offers some sound advice: 'no technology has an impact on learning in its own right; rather, its impact depends upon the way in which it is used' (Luckin et el., 2012: 9). The report itself has lots to say about technology and its use in UK education such as learning from experts, exploring, enquiry and so on – their advice resonates strongly throughout this book.

Whether it is interactive whiteboards, VLEs or mobile devices, the investment in these learning tools is only ever going to have an impact if people are using them and using them well. The Nesta report gives some great case studies on how you can leverage the best return for your investment in terms of learning outcomes for your students.

The confidence and training of teachers plays a large part in the success of any scheme related to the use of technology. In their book *Classroom Dynamics: Implementing a Technology-Based Learning Environment*, Ellen Mandinach and Hugh Cline describe four stages to teachers' use of technology in the classroom (1993: 115):

1. Survival – where teachers are struggling to get to grips with using the technology

2. Mastery – where teachers start to get to grips with the technology and can use it

3. Impact – where teachers can use technology and begin to gain some impact in their use of technology

4. Innovation – where teachers are completely masterful in their use of technology, and innovation and transformation can happen

These basic ideas still hold when considering the use of new technologies by teachers, but in today's society, with the use of technology being so widespread and embedded in the lives of pupils, we are seeing a shift whereby teachers are still the masters of pedagogy, but pupils are the masters of technology.

Boosting the confidence of teaching staff in ICT is therefore crucial. If we use the SAMR model, then we can begin to move forward to a place where lessons are pedagogically sound in their planning: staff still guide pupils in their activities, but pupils self-select from the vast array of tools that are in their mobile learning pencil case. This way of thinking is particularly useful when it comes to considering 'bring your own device' models.

Mobile learning: embrace it

The BYOD model is one which simply asks pupils to bring their own devices to school. This has many whole-school benefits: the cost of the device is not met by the school (saving on those expensive ICT budgets), pupils are able to select their own preferred learning tools and it supports independent learning. However, there are also some downsides. As the device can be anything from a smartphone to a tablet computer, the risk is that teachers are unable to plan effectively for the use of technology in the classroom. In addition, with potentially many different devices in the classroom, the teacher ends up spending a large amount of time troubleshooting tech issues across multiple platforms rather than focusing their time on teaching.

Many educationalists argue that while having access to technology in a BYOD scheme is better than a situation where there is no model at all, BYOD can fail to bring the extended learning benefits that a single device model can offer. When all pupils make use of the same tools, teachers are able to plan lessons more efficiently and thus are able to make much better use of frameworks (e.g. SAMR) to tailor learning experiences. This can lead to transformative learning opportunities that would not have been possible if it were it not for the technology. This, of course, can be possible with BYOD models but it does mean there is the potential for a divide in the classroom between those students who do and do not have devices. It also means, as mentioned above, that the teacher will find it increasingly difficult to plan lessons using specific tools. Effective instructional design in a BYOD model should take on board what Traxler says about students living in a world which is routinely digital. However, this is not always the case.

Alternatively, a 1:1 scheme is one where every pupil in a school is able to use the same learning tool in every lesson on a device which is theirs and that they have access to 24/7. A number of schools across the country now have 1:1 schemes and are finding it to be an extremely beneficial approach to learning for students.

One of the early adopters of a 1:1 scheme was Longfield Academy, in Kent, where the school, working with parents, funded a scheme where every student was given their own iPad. Naace commissioned a report on the students' progress and their findings are compelling: 'There has been a significant and very positive impact on learning and teaching which, in time, should be reflected in achievement and attainment, thanks to both pedagogical changes and new ways of learning engendered by 'any time anywhere' access to information and learning tools' (Heinrich, 2012: 54).

With every student having access to the same device in every lesson and at home, staff are able to plan very effectively and run their courses, assessment, communication and everything else that goes with school life, through the device. This would not be possible in a BYOD environment.

Mobile devices

The standard mobile phone has limited practical application in the classroom, even though it is likely to have an in-built calculator. Your average smartphone, however, is an all-singing, all-dancing device that will have access to an app store that pupils can use to open up a plethora of learning opportunities. Many of the smartphones on the market often have bigger brothers in tablet form which can really start to unlock some fantastic learning opportunities.

With their bigger screens and, generally speaking, better hardware, tablets are appearing in lots of schools, with many more set to come on board. The most popular tablet in schools is currently the iPad, as well as the Samsung Galaxy tablet and iPad mini. A University of Hull research project into Scottish schools and local authorities which have adopted the use of iPads found that 'the adoption of a personalised device significantly transforms access to and use of technology in the classroom'.[3]

Putting mobile technologies into the hands of pupils in your classrooms can help to hit numerous Ofsted descriptors: pupils will have access to a relevant and rich curriculum, they will have the world at their fingertips and this will support outstanding learning and achievement.

In the final section of this chapter we will look at some of the ways that mobile technologies can help you to develop well-judged and inspirational teaching strategies.

---

3   See https://xmascotland.wufoo.eu/forms/scottish-mobile-personal-device-evaluation-2012/

Many headteachers and heads of department or coordinators in improving schools were convinced that the growing use of ICT in a range of subject areas was leading to both increased staff motivation and improved outcomes for pupils. The evidence from this survey suggests that this was the case where ICT was being deployed effectively as part of a strategic approach to the improvement and development of the school.

Ofsted, *ICT in Schools 2008–11* (2011): 46

All-in-one tablets

Among the many reasons why tablets have become so popular in education is the fact that they take technology out of the equation when they are used to demonstrate learning. Apart from the amazing touchscreen on tablets, one of their best features is that they come with lots of in-built devices, including a camera, microphone, keyboard, speakers and screen. Previously, if you wanted pupils to film, record, edit, annotate and wrap it all together, you would need multiple pieces of kit. They would do the filming on one device, then spend time getting the video footage onto another system to enable editing, often hitting difficulties with the compatibility of the video file with the school's system. Pupils would then have to use the complex editing software, which they (or you!) might not know how to use. You would also have to ensure headphones were available.

With a mobile device, all of these functions work seamlessly together to make working with sound and video exceedingly easy. There are lots of services out there – such as YouTube, Vimeo, Edmodo and Google Drive – that are completely free and safe to use, and which give pupils the opportunity to publish their work, gain a (world) wide audience (should you wish it) or a closed audience at home and school. All of these opportunities, and more, are on offer when you choose to embrace mobile technology in your classroom.

AfL using mobile technology

There are a number of tools available (often for free) which enable you to create tests and quizzes for pupils to complete using their devices during a lesson. Popular apps that facilitate this include Google Forms, Socrative and Nearpod. Pupils simply log onto the site, enter your online 'room' and answer the questions. Some tests can be assessed automatically, in which case you can download a completed report for analysis. This will highlight trends and deficits in pupils' knowledge and understanding, enabling you to easily gauge pupil progress and flag up any areas that might need readdressing with the class. A simple, effective and easy tool to master!

Case study

I was keen for my pupils to take more responsibility in meeting the assessment criteria for their controlled assessment. I had set them a revision exercise for homework to carefully read through the criteria. Upon their return to the class, I set them a test using an AfL tool. They accessed this using their mobile devices during the lesson starter. Within five minutes of the students entering the classroom they had all been tested. A report was generated automatically, which I was then able to use to steer the lesson activity to the deficits in their knowledge.

I tested the pupils again at the end of the lesson using similar questions (using the same technique, but in a randomised order). Progress! The pupils' scores were now almost perfect. Using tools such as these in the classroom, and utilising the devices pupils' already have access to, can really shape and hone their knowledge and understanding of various topics.

Case study

Laura Sutherland, an English teacher at Mill Hill School, in London, regularly uses the free AfL tool Socrative as a means of supporting pupil progress in her lessons. She was working with her Year 10 English class who were a few lessons away from their controlled assessment on Priestley's *An Inspector Calls*. For this they would have to write an analytical essay exploring the presentation of community and social prejudice in the play. They had just written their last essay on the text before moving on to their new controlled assessment title, and Laura wanted them to reflect on their work using the GCSE assessment objectives to help them. She also wanted to tackle any key areas of misunderstanding.

Laura used Socrative to draw out their learning. When the students arrived in the classroom they found a simple set of instructions written on the board asking them to take out any internet-enabled device they had with them (an iPad had also been provided for each table of four) and instructing them on how to access Laura's AfL resource. The quiz started with simple right/wrong questions such as:

Which word describes Priestley's political views? A. Capitalist. B. Socialist. C. Communist.

She had previously found that lots of pupils were muddling up these terms in their essays. The questioning facilitated discussion around the room which enabled the pupils to correctly identify definitions. This led to them comparing these political views with the beliefs presented through different characters in *An Inspector Calls*, and thinking about the historical context of the time in which the play was written.

The quiz then moved into broader territory. Each pupil was given AQA controlled assessment mark schemes along with pre-typed example points/paragraphs from their own essays. They were asked questions such as: Which assessment objectives does this paragraph fulfil? They then had to assess the example and discuss it in depth in relation to the criteria. The activity forced pupils to grapple meaningfully with the language of the assessment criteria, thereby deepening their learning objectives and understanding.

The last questions in the quiz asked them to write 'better' versions of some example paragraphs and points using what they had learned and discussed in the lesson. The AfL software enabled all their responses to be saved straight into a spreadsheet when completed. Laura was then able to quickly copy and paste some examples to provide a powerful plenary in which the class considered the strengths of each answer.

All of this might have been possible using traditional methods: Laura could have stood at the front of the classroom and read out the questions, flashing up example paragraphs on an interactive whiteboard or even providing them on a worksheet. The beauty of engaging the pupils with their mobile devices and using Socrative (aside from the novelty value of using a mobile device in class, which should not be dismissed!) was that pupils progressed at their own pace through the questions. They could have as much or as little discussion or debate as they needed, and did not feel pressured by their peers.

The ease and speed with which Laura could manipulate pupils' responses into other formats, and work with them, allowed for much more effective sharing than moving desks around or passing bits of paper about and, above all, it was independent work! Laura only spent 15 minutes preparing the lesson, but spent 50 minutes observing the pupils engage with their learning and with only minimal teacher intervention. As she said herself: 'I facilitated it, they did it.'

Screencasting

Screencasting is a method for recording what happens on your screen. One of the attractions of a tablet device is the touchscreen interface. It makes interacting with them relatively simple – you touch the screen and it responds. Many software developers have capitalised on this and made lots of touch-friendly apps that enable teachers to explain and demonstrate things on the blank canvas of an iPad. Apps such as

ShowMe,[4] ScreenChomp[5] and Explain Everything[6] allow the user to interact with the screen, add images and draw pictures. All the while, every action on the screen is being recorded. Most of these apps record audio at the same time through the built-in microphone.

This gives teachers an exceedingly powerful tool for pupils to demonstrate their knowledge and understanding of any given topic. An example of this was when my pupils created a video featuring a cartoon mole to explain how moles work in chemistry. Students were highly engaged in the activity with the cartoon mole but the level of learning that was going on was transformational. Pupils created highly engaging but factually sound representations of their knowledge and understanding of the topic and thus demonstrated their learning. In addition to this, their videos formed brilliant revision aids ready for their exams.

Research has shown that screencasting can lead to knowledge gains higher than that from live instruction. Katherine Pang of the University of Texas studied the pedagogical effectiveness of multimedia training programmes as compared to traditional face-to-face programmes. She found that 'the video-driven multimedia, web-based instruction was not only pedagogically equivalent in terms of knowledge gains to the live instruction but that the knowledge gains were slightly higher among the web-based participants' (Pang, 2009).

---

4   See https://itunes.apple.com/gb/app/showme-interactive-whiteboard/id445066279?mt=8/

5   See https://itunes.apple.com/gb/app/screenchomp/id442415881?mt=8/

6   See https://itunes.apple.com/gb/app/explain-everything/id431493086?mt=8/

The particle physicist Frank Oppenheimer is widely quoted as saying 'the best way to learn is to teach' which, whilst not based on scientific research, certainly has some roots in pedagogical theory. Certainly, I am not suggesting we ask pupils to teach via a screencast. What I will say, however, is that through the planning, preparation and formulation of their ideas to create a 'good' presentation using one of these tools, pupils are likely to synthesise their knowledge more effectively. Furthermore, once they have produced a number of screencasts about topics on a course, they will have a great library of resources that will help them later on when it comes to exam time and revision.

Green screening

Green screening is a brilliant way of using technology to bring the outside world into the classroom. Also known as chroma keying, it is a special effects technique for layering two video streams or images together based on colour hues. You will probably recognise green screening from seeing the weather on television or from the extras on DVDs where actors stand in front of screens which are later replaced by amazing backgrounds from the film itself.

So what do you need? Firstly, you need a screen that pupils can stand in front of. It doesn't have to be green (blue is also used) but it does seem to work best. You could utilise any wall, perhaps in a foyer or outside a classroom, which has been painted green or blue, or just use a large piece of fabric. Next, you need a device which is capable of recording video and some software which can remove the green screen in the finished video. This kind of work is going on in lots of schools and, despite sounding like the stuff of Hollywood, there are apps available that can do this for as little as £1.49.[7]

The benefits of working with video are extensive. If we think back to the discussions about SAMR in Chapter 1, there are learning opportunities here that would not have been possible if it were not for this new technology. Therefore, you are using strategies in your classroom that are transforming how the learning is taking place.

Consider the sorts of activities that could now transpire:

- A pupil could film a news report from outside 10 Downing Street
- A geography report on volcanoes could be filmed on the side of a volcano that was actually spewing molten rock
- A music recital could appear as if it was taking place on a stage in front of a massive crowd at Glastonbury
- An art work could be explained to an audience from inside Tate Britain
- A maths explanation could be given on the set of *Blue Peter*

Backgrounds can easily be found for your creative ideas by doing a Google image search or exploring other great sites such as Flickr – the possibilities are endless. By making the

---

7   For example, the Green Screen Movie FX app: https://itunes.apple.com/gb/app/green-screen-movie-fx/id445285983?mt=8/

task transformational for your pupils, then the learning should be transformational too.

iTunes U

One of the areas in which Apple have invested heavily is their iTunes U service, which was designed to make educational audio and video content from leading colleges and universities available as an app.[8] Prestigious universities such as Harvard and the Massachusetts Institute of Technology (MIT), as well as smaller schools and state districts, have made thousands of courses available on iTunes U, including lectures and lecture notes, texts and tests. Education Scotland even offers courses in Gaelic and English. Resources for Early Years education are also available. By adding their own courses to the site, schools can create their own resources for pupils via the iTunes U Course Manager.[9] Pupils can access this content at any time on their devices, given the right permissions from their teacher.

Making use of all of these resources can really support learning outside of the (flipped) classroom. The courses are also downloadable, so as long as pupils have access to a mobile device, they don't need to have internet access at home to use them. These resources work in a very similar way to the books in the iBooks app, albeit they are set out a little differently.

---

8   The iTunes U app for iPad, iPhone and iPod touch can be accessed for free at https://itunes.apple.com/gb/app/itunes-u/id490217893?mt=8/
9   Find out more at http://www.apple.com/uk/support/itunes-u/course-manager/

Case study

iTunes U has been utilised at Clevedon School, in Bristol, for the A level computing course, where pupils' learning was enriched by MIT's course 'Introduction to Algorithms'. After the teacher had delivered the course, pupils were given the opportunity to see what further learning in this area would be like at a university level, which also helped to raise their aspirations. They were excited by the prospects that furthering their studies in this particular area could bring. Inspired by using the iTunes U app, some of the pupils downloaded the entire course and have furthered their learning by completing various aspects of the online course.

Top tips

■ Embrace the use of mobile technologies within your school and exploit the opportunities they can bring for transformational and inspirational teaching and learning.

■ Take time to carefully consider the model (BYOD vs. 1:1 or a mixture) and financing that are best suited to your school and pupils.

■ If you are just embarking on this journey, reach out to those schools that have already implemented mobile technologies and learn from their experiences – perhaps see what free training is available (e.g. a local TeachMeet event).

■ Publish your courses to iTunes U or simply make use of the vast range of resources already available.

■ Consider the use of green screen technology to bring about new learning opportunities.

■ Further reinforce learning by asking pupils to create their own 'flipped' resources using touchscreen apps, such as Explain Everything.

Chapter 6

Literacy, digital literacy and ICT

In some of the schools, ICT was used effectively to engage boys more successfully in English, especially in reading and writing. These pupils were motivated to improve their reading skills to enable them to understand and report on material researched on the internet.

Ofsted, *ICT in Schools 2008–11* (2011): 10

In this chapter we will consider what digital literacy means and explore some tools and activities to support it. We will also look at how to use search engines efficiently and consider how technology can be used to improve feedback and proofreading.

Digital literacy

Literacy – that is reading, writing, oracy and critical thinking – is one of the core skills that should pervade every aspect of every subject in school. However, I believe that *digital literacy* should also have this core skill status. It signifies much more than simply a combination of the two terms, *digital* and *literacy*. By digital literacy, I mean the capacity to understand, assess, transform and create information using a range of digital media.

Digital literacy does not replace traditional reading and writing skills, but it does build upon them. A pupil who is digitally literate is one who is able to effectively and critically navigate, create, process, evaluate and communicate information using a range of different digital techniques. The ability to scan, skim and disseminate information, for example, which are found within literacy, are also skills within digital literacy. It requires pupils to be able to practise these skills using a wide range of technologies.

Digital literacy is not only about pupils being able to use a computer but requires them to use technology effectively to find information and then to be critical of its authenticity: '21st century literacy is the set of abilities and skills where aural, visual and digital literacy overlap. These include the ability to understand the power of images and sounds, to recognize and use that power, to manipulate and transform digital media, to distribute them pervasively' (New Media Consortium, 2005: 2).

A report by National Literacy Trust, *Young People's Writing: Attitudes, Behaviour and the Role of Technology*, which was based on a survey of children aged from 9 to 16, found that 24% were blogging and 73% were using technology to communicate in writing using tools such as online messaging services (Clark and Dugdale, 2009). Interestingly, of the children who neither blogged nor used social networking, only 47% rated their writing as 'good' or 'very good', whereas 61% of the bloggers and 56% of the social networkers said the same. The report suggests that there is a strong correlation between pupils using technology and wider patterns of reading and writing, meaning that the more you can get pupils to use technology for reading and written communication, the more likely it is that these skills will improve. Jonathan Douglas of the National Literacy Trust suggests that rather than damaging literacy, 'the more forms of communications children use the stronger their core literacy skills' (quoted in Kleinman, 2009).

Search engines

Search engines are fantastic tools to help us search for and find information. Ian Gilbert uses the pertinent question that pupils often ask in the title of his brilliant book, *Why Do I Need a Teacher When I've Got Google?* (2010). Well, if you're not using a search engine properly, you can find yourself failing to find the information you want or not exploiting that knowledge to the full.

Search engines work using Boolean logic, which involves using double quote marks to specify words or phrases and the minus sign (-) in order to make your searches more specific. The tips below should help you and your pupils make the most of Google and other search engines.

Specific phrases

Rather than searching for *monarchs of England*, which would give results from sites that contain all these words, search more specifically by putting the phrase in double quotes:

"monarchs of England"

This will bring up search results that include the specific phrase.

Exclude words

Sometimes when you are searching for a term, a number of results might include words that you don't want in your search results. You can exclude them by adding the word you do not want in your search with a minus sign in front of it. For example:

"monarchs of England" -battle -war -wives

Site-specific searches

There could be times when you want to search a specific website for a phrase. This can be done in this way:

"monarchs of England" site: www.britishlibrary.co.uk

Specific document types

Sometimes you might want to search for resources based on specific document types. For example, to search for a PowerPoint presentation, type:

"monarchs of England" filetype:ppt

This will locate PowerPoint presentations that contain the term 'monarchs of England'. Knowing about different file type extensions will help you to do this, so here is a list of popular file types and their extensions:

- Word documents: doc or docx
- Excel documents: xls or xlsx
- PowerPoint documents: ppt or pptx
- PDF files: PDF
- Images: jpg, tiff or png
- Videos: mp4, avi or mpg
- Audio: wav or mp3

Definitions

You can also use search engines to find definitions. Simply type in the search operator 'define' followed by the word you want defining. For example:

Define: undergirded

Number ranges

Number range searches are particularly useful when you are looking for results that contain information from within specific date ranges. For example, if you wanted to find out about monarchs between 1066 and 1850 you can search using the X..Y sequence, where between the X and the Y value there are two full stops. For example:

"monarchs of England" 1066..1850

Calculator

The next time you need to do a sum, simply type it into Google using the +, -, * and / characters for addition, subtraction, multiplication and division. For example:

*541318.864 * 32.2457*

Chapter 6

Software features to assist with literacy

Annotation tools

Annotating work is something we do all the time as teachers when marking books. We can do this kind of annotation using technology too.

PDF (Portable Document Format) editors, such as Adobe Acrobat, are free to download.[1] Annotating a PDF is a great way to encourage pupils to edit and review documents. Tools normally available with annotation software include:

- Highlighters
- Speech bubbles
- Add/remove pages
- Share comments and annotations
- Proofreading mark-ups

Tools such as Showbie[2] can be used quickly and easily by pupils with tablets, and it is certainly easier and a lot cheaper to share a PDF document with pupils rather than printing it out and distributing it to the class. How many times have you heard pupils complain that they have messed up their sheet and want to start again? With a PDF, they can simply erase any mistakes and resume.

---

1   See http://www.adobe.com/Acrobat_XI/
2   See https://itunes.apple.com/us/app/showbie-collect-review-annotate/
    id548898085?mt=8/

PDF editors are very handy tools for teachers too. Editing a downloaded PDF was previously quite difficult to master. With PDF editing/annotation tools, you can strip away the sections of the document that you don't want and leave yourself with the bits that you do. This is very helpful when creating bespoke resources from a variety of other sources you might have compiled.

Feedback and proofreading

Many schools have a proofreading code, where students are asked to check their spelling, punctuation and grammar before submitting their work. When work is completed using a word processor, there is no excuse for pupils not spell checking it.

With more and more pupils turning to electronic devices to create their work, particularly word processors for written work, review tools can be a very powerful and supportive way to give feedback to pupils.

One of the greatest features for supporting literacy using ICT is the reviewing tool often found in word processors. The review tool (e.g. in Microsoft Word) enables you to annotate work pupils have sent to you, make comments and suggest references and pointers for improvement. The pupil can then review these comments one by one when they receive the work back and action them as appropriate. The software tracks all of the changes made and so a timeline of changes is created.

As part of this process, a file will be sent to and fro between the teacher and pupil, creating an organic document that may be updated and revised many times over. However, it is imperative that you retain a means of evidencing that the work has been marked and feedback given, as comments and tracked changes will be obliterated from the working version once they are accepted or rejected by the pupil. This can be done by saving the file with a different name (e.g. filename v1, filename v2) each time you save it, which will enable you to preserve previous versions.

It is not within the scope of this book to describe the importance of assessment and feedback. However, if you are reliant on technology, it is important that you make sure that the systems you have in place are transparent. If you have a VLE at your school then this should be a relatively easy process.

Activities to support literacy

Ofsted's *Moving English Forward* report clearly recognises the power of ICT to support literacy, as in this example from one school:

The use of ICT and media technology is a key strength in teaching and learning. In every class there were impressive examples of how this had supported students' understanding of, and enthusiasm for, English. Particularly effective examples included:

- an online newspaper written by pupils
- animations written, directed and produced by pupils
- radio plays written, directed and acted by pupils, including one based on *Macbeth*
- homework emailed to teachers
- video conferencing involving local authors and pupils in other local schools.

Ofsted, *Moving English Forward* (2012): 22

We have already looked at a number of strategies that support literacy (e.g. blogging in Chapter 3). Here are some other suggestions.

Chapter 6

Newspapers

Using collaborative software and email to send work backwards and forwards between pupils and teachers is one way to build articles for a newspaper. There are various tools available to make this possible. As already mentioned, Google Drive allows pupils to work together in real time on a word-processed document, but there many other ways to do this. Microsoft's Publisher, for example, is available in most schools and does an admirable job of creating a professional looking school newspaper using tools such as frames, text boxes and wraparound images.

One possible pitfall here is that you don't necessarily want pupils to be spending lots of time designing a layout or considering what fonts to choose, when what you want them to be focusing on is literacy and subject content. Use the following tips to keep the focus on their writing:

- Tell pupils the audience for their newspaper
- Give them a front page template
- Set out the text boxes where you want them
- Inform pupils which font you want them to use and what size headings and body text should be
- Create spaces where you want the images to be positioned and make space for a caption box under each photo
- Let pupils know that you don't want any blank space in the text boxes

This last point will ensure that pupils write enough and will also see them refining their text, thinking about their language and considering their audience. This ties in well with another comment from Ofsted regarding language use and context:

[M]ost pupils are regular users of, and effective managers of, modern digital technology. Teachers need to use these contexts in their lessons if learning in English is not to seem out of step with pupils' experiences, but also to enable them to make appropriate style and language choices when using different media and communication forms.

Ofsted, *Moving English Forward* (2012): 53

Animations

You might be wondering how creating animations can support literacy and help to improve written English. It does so through the process of creating the animations. Planning and storyboarding the stages of the animation and the discussion required among the pupils to produce the animation require high levels of precision in both oral and written communication.

There are different ways to create stop-motion animations, along the lines of *Wallace and Gromit*, in which you take a photo of every frame of movement then edit them together.

There are lots of tools that can support this kind of activity. Zu3D[3] is very popular in primary schools and has various useful features. I Can Animate[4] is another popular tool and works on multiple platforms.

As always, remember not to focus on the technology but on the learning – the literacy shown in oral and written communication.

Radio plays and podcasts

In *Moving English Forward*, Ofsted suggest that radio plays are an effective way of supporting literacy (2012: 22). Podcasting offers a similar way to support literacy through the use of ICT. A podcast is an audio file that has been created using technology which can contain any kind of audio and is often shared once completed. Ensure that pupils understand fully how they will use the technology in the tasks they are given. For example, ask them to:

▨ Plan their podcast

▨ Write the script

▨ Gain peer feedback in a 'critical friend' fashion (kind, specific and helpful)

▨ Record their podcast

▨ Share it with the world!

---

3 See http://www.zu3d.com/
4 See http://www.kudlian.net/products/icananimate/

There are many different ways to record a podcast. The use of tablet and mobile technology makes this increasingly easy and there are numerous free applications which make this possible. SoundCloud and Audioboo, for example, are free tools for use on iPad and Android tablets which you can use via their websites or from free apps available at the Apple App or Google Play stores. Both tools offer users free access to sharing recorded information online.[5] All you need to do is load the app, fill in the required fields (such as a name to distinguish your recording) and away you go! When completed, the recording will be uploaded to your Audioboo site and can be listened back to on any internet-enabled device.

Podcasts are a great way to record:

- Notes for the class
- Feedback or comments on pupils' work
- Learning conversations
- Spoken presentations or other oracy work by pupils
- Stories

---

5   Visit http://bit.ly/audiobooexample to hear a short clip of me using Audioboo.

Case study[6]

A great example of how ICT can be used to support literacy is a digital literacy storytelling project created by Sheli Blackburn of Roydon Primary School, in Norfolk, in conjunction with the University of East Anglia. It was a project inspired by Kate Pullinger's *Inanimate Alice*, a digital novel set in a technology-augmented near-future.

The work involved pupils collecting digital assets (e.g. photographs, videos) from a trip to the local fen. The items were brought back to school and used in a variety of different ways, such as being animated or added to videos to make digital storybooks. Once the stories had been created they were added to a class map on their Google account.[7] This was then shared with parents, who could view the work by visiting the map and clicking on the different icons. Each icon represented a unique story created by a pupil in Sheli's class.

Homework emailed to teachers

Email is a fantastic communication medium and provides an opportunity for teachers to have a learning dialogue with

---

6   Sheli's finished project can be found at http://carryonlearning.blogspot.co.uk/search/label/UEA%20project/

7   It is important to note that the Google accounts described here are only possible through the use of Google Apps for Education. More information on this can be found at http://www.google.com/enterprise/apps/education/

pupils about their work. It is paperless, so you don't have to carry it around, it is easily accessible from lots of devices and it's not going to be lost (or eaten by the dog!). However, be sure to ask pupils to follow a specific framework when submitting their work to you. For example, ask them to ensure that the email has:

- A subject line
- A salutation
- A clearly explained purpose for the email
- A complimentary close
- It has been spell checked and proofread before sending

Also insist that any attached written work is also spell checked and proofread. By following these simple steps, pupils will have to think more carefully about their use of language and its presentation. There is also the added bonus that you won't have to guess the intent of their email.

If you want to focus specifically on feedback in pupil work submissions, then you could provide them with a template which they can copy and paste into their emails. Asking pupils to complete a writing frame (such as the example opposite) can really help them to develop a deeper level of thinking and understanding of their learning process than would have otherwise taken place. Note that the framework has blank spaces for the teacher to reply in which enables there to be a conversation about the learning.

Your feedback

WWW – What Went Well

Please write in this section at least three sentences highlighting what went well in this piece of work.

The best piece of my work was ...

The bit I am most proud of is ...

I worked best in this piece of work when ...

EBI – Even Better If

Please write in this section at least three sentences highlighting what you could have done to make your submitted work even better.

My work would have been better if ...

I could have made more progress with my work if ...

I could improve on similar tasks in the future by ...

Effort	😊	😐	☹

[Teacher comments here]

Quality of outcome	😊	😐	☹️
[Teacher comments here]			

Peer feedback – delete the notes below when entering your peer feedback

Critique – please collect feedback from another pupil in the group that is *kind*, *specific* and *helpful* so that you can improve your work and resubmit it.

Pupil feedback (fill in this section and forward this to your class teacher)

Taking into account all of the feedback above, please improve your first submission. Then resubmit your work clearly marked FINAL DRAFT.

Write in this section what you did to improve your submission:

Top tips

■ Optimise results by skilled use of search engines.

■ Use review tools in word processors to refine work.

■ Use annotation tools on touch devices to leave written feedback on typed work.

■ Use technology to engage in learning conversations.

■ Use technology to provide writing frames for pupils to sharpen their focus on the task and their learning.

■ Have high expectations of pupils' literacy when using technology by creating clear rules for the presentation of written work.

■ Create podcasts and give pupils an extra audience by publishing them online.

Chapter 7

Social media

When people are asked what they think social media is, many will reply, 'Well, it's Facebook, isn't it?' Ask teachers further about how they're using social media in their classrooms and they often look blank or puzzled. Many schools have banned sites like Facebook, YouTube and Twitter, sometimes for good reason, but in fact these tools can support, enhance and transform existing learning and can make a wealth of new learning opportunities available. As outstanding teachers, we should look to capitalise on them – not just for the pupils but for ourselves as well. E-safety is, of course, absolutely key, but the potential benefits of social media, properly handled, can far outweigh the risks.

Twitter

The use of social media can bring some fantastic opportunities for your own professional development as well as for your pupils, school and more. As mentioned in Chapter 4 on e-safety, ensuring you are safe online is of paramount importance. Take on board the advice given in this chapter, and throughout this book, and stick to it. If in doubt, seek advice.

Teachers who use Twitter regularly say that it's simply the best CPD they've ever had and that it's like the best staffroom in the world. By 'following' other teaching professionals on Twitter, you'll find that, without having to type any messages yourself, each time you log on, you will be presented with inspiration after inspiration.

Take, for example, the superb Tom Sherrington, head teacher of King Edward VI Grammar School in Chelmsford, Essex[1] **@headguruteacher**. On any given day he will be offering not only his own pearls of wisdom in tweet fashion, but also links to his insightful blog[2] and other teaching resources and relevant articles. If you tweet him, he will probably reply. As you increase the number of people that you follow, so you will begin to develop your own professional learning network (PLN).

How to set up a PLN

An educational professional (or personal) learning network is a group of teachers and educators who interact using social media, usually Twitter, to share, learn and develop ideas across a social media platform.

---

1   See https://twitter.com/KEGS_Chelmsford/
2   See http://headguruteacher.com/

The best way to go about setting up your own PLN is to go to Twitter and start searching for key words. For example, if you are a primary school teacher looking to find other teachers and resources related to primary education, a search for 'primary ICT' would bring up results from people linked to primary education and ICT. When I performed this search, I found resources and blogs linked to primary ICT, a primary Ofsted inspector with a specialism in ICT and someone talking about Naace, the UK's National Association of Advisors for Computers in Education.

Within a PLN there is no expectation that you have to engage with any of the individuals you follow. In fact, many teachers follow people on Twitter and simply get ideas from what they are saying and the links they are posting. It is very often the case that topics for discussion are seasonal and so are very current. For example, between March and June, expect lots of debate and discussion about learning techniques related to revision, controlled assessments, testing and examinations. When something happens of global or national significance – for example, a national curriculum review – expect teachers to be discussing items related to that, either generally or by subject. An ongoing example of this would be the discussions that take place on Twitter based around the hashtag #ukedchat. Searching for this hashtag brings up tweets containing that hashtag but also comments related to education in the UK.

If you are looking for daily ICT inspiration, why not follow the brilliant Tim Rylands **@timrylands**? An award-winning primary teacher with 25 years of teaching experience, Tim puts up an inspiring tool or reference to exciting technology every day on Twitter and in his blog.[3] Like Tom Sherrington, Tim interacts with teachers from around the world using social media, particularly on Twitter.

By developing your own PLN you are one step towards gaining extra confidence in using new technology in ways you had not previously thought possible. In his article, 'The Ten Stages of Twitter' (2012), teacher Daniel Edwards **@syded06** recreates the stages that many teachers go through when they sign up to Twitter. It's true that many people who first sign up will follow Stephen Fry and wonder what the fuss is all about. Sticking with it though can bring about some fantastic learning opportunities. As mentioned above, many teachers refer to Twitter as being the best staffroom in the world and there is a good reason for this: it is full of teachers who work hard every day for the best results for the pupils in their care. Twitter is like a staffroom where people are still discussing learning ideas at 11 o'clock at night in their holidays! They are certainly not those that Chief Inspector Sir Michael Wilshaw refers to as being out 'of the gate at 3 o'clock' (Hurst and Treneman, 2012). These teachers exist, but you aren't one of them – you wouldn't be reading this book if you were!

If you are new to Twitter, here are a few Twitterisms that you may find helpful.

---

3   See http://www.timrylands.com/

Twitterisms

Tweet	A message on Twitter, limited to 140 characters.
Timeline	This is the main area on Twitter where you will see all of the tweets written by the various people that you follow.
Twitter ID	Someone's name on Twitter (e.g. my ID is **@ICTEvangelist** and the editor's ID is **@jackiebeere**).
Follower	This is someone who follows your Twitter ID and reads the things you say.
Connect	This is the area where you will find information about any tweets that have been written that include your Twitter ID (e.g. when someone has re-tweeted one of your tweets to their followers). Alternatively, if someone has mentioned your name in a tweet, perhaps in response to a tweet you have written, this is where you will see it.
Avi or Avatar	A small image used to represent you in your profile. This normally appears alongside your tweets. When you first sign up to Twitter you will be assigned an avi of an egg. In my experience, many teachers on Twitter will not interact with a user with an egg as their avi.
Profile	This is a short piece of text (again limited in terms of characters) where you explain who you are and what you're doing on Twitter.

Favorite[4]	A Favorite is a tweet that you might want to refer back to later. If you 'Favorite' a tweet, you will be able to go back to it at a later stage quickly and easily.[5]
Hashtag	This is anything that has been written within a tweet that starts with a hashtag (#) symbol. They are searchable and clickable. Clicking on a hashtag will bring up all tweets that contain that hashtag. Popular examples are #ukedchat or globally #edchat (more on these below).
RT	A tweet that has been 're-tweeted' to share or to show agreement with the original tweet.
MT	Modified tweet. A tweet that has been re-tweeted but modified or added to in some way.
TT	A tweet that has been translated. Often written so that inconsistencies in direct translation can be recognised and to clarify meaning.
DM	Direct message. This is a message sent directly to you which is private. It will not appear on the timeline. You can only send DM's to people who follow you and vice versa.
NSFW	Not suitable for work. If you see this in a tweet, be careful – it probably contains a link or images unsuitable for general public consumption!
TIL	Today I learned (e.g. 'TIL that the acronym NSFW stands for not suitable for work!').

4   Please excuse the American spelling!
5   When you can't remember the name of that fantastic resource you are trying to tell your colleague about in the staffroom, jump straight to your Favorites and let them see (a) how easy Twitter is to use, (b) how great your resource is and c) how amazing you are (even if it's a resource you've magpied!).

Chapter 7

Hashtags

As mentioned above, hashtags are words that are used within tweets that start with the # symbol. This makes them searchable and will normally group like-minded people and their tweets together. Tweets containing hashtags are currently only searchable for a period of 14 days although the original tweets will be still be on the profile of the person who wrote them.

Across the world, teachers use hashtags to group topical points together under one hashtag. A very popular hashtag in UK education discussions is #ukedchat. This is an online discussion that takes place every Thursday night. It has been running for a number of years and there is a synopsis of every chat and its topic on the website at http://ukedchat. com/. Each week a topic is put out to a poll on the website and participants are asked to vote on what current education issues they may want to discuss and then, on Thursday night from 8–9 p.m., the topic is discussed. Issues addressed include anything from general education to literacy, ICT across the curriculum, AfL strategies and many more.

Even if you are a bit unsure about the prospect of using Twitter to tweet yourself, the site alone is a great resource for learning new ways to improve your practice. Also, if you are looking to find good people to follow on Twitter, many of the best will feature heavily in educational discussions and many share their resources too. Twitter is swiftly becoming the essential tool for every teacher to access for professional development.

Here is a list of useful education-related hashtags. It is by no means exhaustive – you can see how many there are by simply Googling 'educational hashtags'.

Education-related hashtags

#ukedchat	UK-based education discussion
#addcym	The Welsh equivalent of #ukedchat
#edchat	The global equivalent of #ukedchat
#satchat	A US-based Saturday equivalent of #ukedchat
#edtech	Educational technology
#iPaded	iPad education topics
#pedagoo	Scottish pedagogy organisation Pedagoo
#pedagoofriday	The best thing that has happened in your classroom that week – great to read at the end of a busy week
#collabed	Collaborative education
#engchat	English curriculum discussions
#learning	Learning topics
#mlearning	Mobile learning
#asechat	Science education
#stem	The STEM curriculum
#education	Education

Chapter 7

Using social media as a school

More schools are embracing the use of social media like Twitter within their communities. It can be an important avenue of communication for parents and pupils. For example, schools and departments use social media to pass on inspirational messages, information about coursework deadlines, timely reminders, links to related work and to share success. Three good examples of schools that are tweeting are Clevedon School in Bristol **@ClevedonSchool**, Davyhulme Primary School in Manchester **@DavyhulmePS** and Calderstones (secondary) School in Liverpool **@CaldiesTandL**.

However, if you are thinking that this could be a fantastic and quick way for your school or department to communicate with your community – don't just jump in. There are a few simple, best practice rules you should follow:

- Create a very clear policy on the use of social media by staff
- Set up a Twitter account especially for the purpose
- Create a memorable user name – for example, if your school is Anytown High School, then **@Anytownhigh** would be a good name. If you're a business studies department, then **@AntownhighBusiness** might be a good option
- Do not tweet parents and pupils from your personal account and do not follow back
- Do not engage in conversations with parents or pupils – simply use them as a one-way information feed

- Do not tweet pupils' full names
- If posting photos of pupils, ensure that you have parental permission to do so
- Update your tweets regularly – if you are going to use it as a means of communication and want the community to engage with it, it needs to be used on a regular basis
- The best way to use Twitter as a means of communication and engagement is to embed it in your teaching

Other social media

Twitter is not the only type of social media that can help teachers to access, share and develop resources and communicate with the school community. There are lots of possibilities to build new communication channels with pupils, colleagues and parents, such as Facebook and Pinterest, and these can be very exciting. However, before embarking on using any new social media publicly as a school, consider:

- Who will update it?
- What will your rules be?
- How will your pupils/staff/parents use it?
- Are your pupils/staff/parents already using it, and how?
- Does it have e-safety issues associated with it?
- What benefits will it bring to communication and learning?

If you bear these key points in mind, and make sure that the use of the social media is manageable and that it brings wins for you or your school community, then it is definitely worth exploring.

Facebook

Facebook offers a service called Groups for Schools which allows schools to set up their own pages and spaces as a means to communicate with the community. As with Twitter, some common sense, best practice rules should apply:

Do:

- Regularly post success stories and items about learning happening in your school/department/lesson/ tutor group. If the page is for a tutor group, you can post birthday wishes (although remember not to miss anyone out!)

- As with Twitter, set up a separate page for your school presence – do not use your personal account. It could be Anytown High, or History Anytown High, depending on whether you're a school or department. If you're setting up a teacher account you could perhaps call it Anytown High Anderson or ICT Anytown High Anderson

- Make sure that any group pages are closed and that individuals have to request to join – that way, only the people you wish to see the group pages can do so

- Keep your personal pages and your school/professional pages very separate
- Post update messages in Facebook onto the timeline to remind students or parents of any deadlines that are coming up or of any last minute changes

Don't:

- View pupils' photos
- Send or respond to private messages
- Use Facebook chat – it is not appropriate
- 'Friend' pupils or parents
- Make negative comments

These guidelines are intended to serve as a useful reference but are not exhaustive. You should satisfy yourself as to what best practice is at any given time because Facebook updates its privacy policies regularly (a feature that this printed book unfortunately lacks!).[6]

Pinterest

Pinterest is a relatively new but popular social media site where members can collect and organise resources. As a vehicle for sharing educational resources, it is proving to have a big impact in various areas, such as:

- Helping teachers with their planning

---

6   Juliette and Stephen Heppell (2010) have written a useful article on the ways in which Facebook can be used by schools, which is available at http://www.heppell.net/facebook_in_school/

■ Sharing resources amongst teachers

■ Sharing resources with pupils

■ Curating your own resources

■ Accessing the quality resources of others

To use Pinterest, simply visit www.pinterest.com or download the Pinterest app to your device and search for what you are looking for using the search facility. Then scroll through the resources that you can find. Users of Pinterest classify their various 'pins' using 'boards', so on a particular board you will find resources connected to that particular topic. It is particularly useful for finding inspiration on wall displays, lesson plans, topic ideas, infographics[7] and CPD resources.

You can use Pinterest to:

■ Organise your own resources

■ Promote your own work

■ Swap lesson plans

■ Get feedback on your ideas

■ Share resources with your pupils for a particular topic

■ Stay on top of current trends

In summary, the use of Twitter is highly recommended as a means to expand your continuing professional development – and it is easy to use. Although the terminology can initially

---

7   An infographic is a graphic design that incorporates data, which is represented in a variety of charts alongside related information. Infographics are normally very clear and quite beautiful representations of data.

be daunting, by using the information provided in this chapter you will be able to use it without difficulty. Other social media sites can also bring about opportunities to inspire and engage both you and your pupils.

Top tips

- Have a school policy on best use of social media.
- Use Twitter as a CPD tool.
- Set up a department Facebook page.
- Use Pinterest either as a tool for your CPD or as a sharing tool with classes.
- Choose a sensible name linked to your subject, role or school.
- Only post things you would not mind your head teacher reading.
- Learn lots from others.
- Share back (when you're ready!).

And finally ...

At the start of this book, I talked about taking fears and turning them into confidence. Throughout the book I have endeavoured to give examples of how you can take technology and leverage it to bring about powerful learning opportunities for you and your pupils. I strongly advocate getting yourself onto Twitter as a means to further your network of colleagues and to use it to begin to read the blogs of other teachers who are on the same journey as you – dedicated professionals wanting to improve the teaching and learning that goes on in their classrooms.

Whilst I haven't given you hard and fast rules, please take from this book the power, the belief and the imperative that you can give all of these ideas a go and make them work for you in whatever setting you are in. Whether primary, secondary or further education, we can all learn from each other – just take these ideas and try them in your classroom! I look forward to hearing about how you and your pupils are transforming learning through the use of technology.

Thank you for reading and if you want to find out more, follow me on Twitter **@ICTevangelist**

Bibliography and further reading
All websites correct as of 26 August 2013.

Beadle, Phil (2010). *How to Teach*. Carmarthen: Crown House Publishing.

Biggs, John B. and Collis, Kevin F. (1982). *Evaluating the Quality of Learning: The SOLO Taxonomy* (Educational Psychology Series). New York: Academic Press.

Chohan, Abdul (2012). 'Case Study: iPods and Apps at Essa Academy'. Available at: http://www.innovatemyschool.com/industry-expert-articles/item/284-case-study-ipods-and-apps-at-essa-academy.html/

Clark, Christina and Dugdale, George (2009). *Young People's Writing: Attitudes, Behaviour and the Role of Technology*. Available at: http://www.literacytrust.org.uk/assets/0000/0226/Writing_survey_2009.pdf/

Claxton, Guy, Chambers, Maryl, Powell, Graham and Lucas, Bill (2011). *The Learning Powered School*. Bristol: TLO.

Coles, Tait (2012a). 'SOLO Stations'. Available at: http://taitcoles.wordpress.com/2012/05/08/solo-stations/

Coles, Tait (2012b). 'SOLO Taxonomy and RealSmart'. Available at: http://taitcoles.wordpress.com/2012/09/23/solo-taxonomy-and-realsmart/

DfE (2013). 'Consultation on Computing and Disapplication of the Current National Curriculum'. Available at: http://www.education.gov.uk/schools/teachingandlearning/curriculum/nationalcurriculum2014/a00224578/consultation/

Didau, David (2012). *The Perfect Ofsted English Lesson*. Carmarthen: Independent Thinking Press.

Digital Classroom Teaching Task and Finish Group (2012). *Find It, Make It, Use It, Share It: Learning in Digital Wales*. Ref: CAD/GM/0213. Available at: http://www.learn-ict.org.uk/resources/self_review/docs/findit-makeit-useit.pdf/

Bibliography and further reading

DiNucci, Darci (1999). 'Fragmented Future', *Print* magazine. Available at http://www.darcyd.com/fragmented_future.pdf/

Edwards, Daniel (2012). 'Teachers: The 10 Stages of Twitter'. Available at: http://syded.wordpress.com/2012/06/13/teachers-the-10-stages-of-twitter/

Facer, Keri (2011). *Learning Futures: Education, Technology and Social Change*. Abingdon and New York: Routledge.

Gilbert, Ian (2007). *The Little Book of Thunks*. Carmarthen: Crown House Publishing.

Gilbert, Ian (2010). *Why Do I Need A Teacher When I've Got Google?* Abingdon and New York: Routledge.

Glisksman, Sam (2013). *iPad in Education for Dummies*. Hoboken, NJ: John Wiley & Sons.

Hattie, John (1999). 'Influences on Student Learning'. Lecture delivered at the University of Auckland, 2 August. Available at: http://www.teacherstoolbox.co.uk/downloads/managers/Influencesonstudent.pdf/

Hattie, John (2012). *Visible Learning for Teachers: Maximising Impact on Learning* (Kindle edition). London and New York: Routledge.

Heinrich, Paul (2012). *The iPad as a Tool for Education: A Study of the Introduction of iPads at Longfield Academy, Kent*. Available at: http://www.naace.co.uk/get.html?_Action=GetFile&_Key=Data26613&_Id=1965&_Wizard=0&_DontCache=1341555048/

Heppell, Juliette and Heppell, Stephen (2010). 'Using Facebook in the Classroom'. Available at: http://www.heppell.net/facebook_in_school/

Hook, Pam (2011). 'SOLO Taxonomy'. Available at: http://pamhook.com/solo-taxonomy/

Hurst, Greg and Treneman, Ann (2012). 'Stay On After School If You Want Pay Rise, Teachers Told'. Available at: http://www.thetimes.co.uk/tto/education/article3546544.ece/

Jenkins, Henry, *Confronting the Challenges of Participatory Culture: Media Education for the 21st Century*. Cambridge, MA: MIT Press.

Khan, Salman (2011). 'Let's Use Video to Reinvent Education' [video]. Available at: http://www.ted.com/talks/salman_khan_let_s_use_video_to_reinvent_education.html/

Bibliography and further reading

Kleinman, Zoe (2009). 'Children Who Use Technology Are "Better Writers"'. Available at: http://news.bbc.co.uk/1/hi/technology/8392653.stm/

Luckin, Rosemary, Bligh, Brett, Manches, Andrew, Ainsworth, Shaaron, Crook, Charles and Noss, Richard (2012). *Decoding Learning: The Proof, Promise and Potential of Digital Education*. Available at: http://www.nesta.org.uk/library/documents/DecodingLearningReport_v12.pdf/

McLoughlin, Simon (2011). 'Skype in My Classroom'. Available at: http://simcloughlin.com/skype-in-my-classroom/

Mandinach, Ellen B. and Cline, Hugh F. (1993). *Classroom Dynamics: Implementing a Technology-Based Learning Environment*. Hillsdale, NJ: Routledge.

Meeker, Mary, Devitt, Scott and Wu, Liang (2012). *Internet Trends*. Available at: http://www.scribd.com/document_downloads/29850507?extension=pdf&from=embed&source=embed/

New Media Consortium (2005). *A Global Imperative: The Report of the 21st Century Literacy Summit*. Available at: http://www.nmc.org/pdf/Global_Imperative.pdf/

O'Reilly, Tim (2005). 'What Is Web 2.0: Design Patterns and Business Models for the Next Generation of Software'. Available at: http://oreilly.com/web2/archive/what-is-web-20.html/

Ofsted (2009a). *The Importance of ICT: Information and Communication Technology in Primary and Secondary Schools, 2005/2008*. Ref: 070035. Available at: http://www.ofsted.gov.uk/resources/importance-of-ict-information-and-communication-technology-primary-and-secondary-schools-20052008/

Ofsted (2009b). *The Safe Use of New Technologies*. Ref: 090231. Available at: http://www.ofsted.gov.uk/sites/default/files/documents/surveys-and-good-practice/t/The%20safe%20use%20of%20new%20technologies.pdf/

Ofsted (2011). *ICT in schools 2008–11*. Ref: 110134. Available at: http://www.ofsted.gov.uk/resources/ict-schools-2008-11/

Ofsted (2012a). *The Evaluation Schedule for the Inspection of Maintained Schools and Academies*. Ref: 090095. London: Ofsted.

Ofsted (2012b). *Haworth Primary School: Inspection Report No. 377559*. Available at: http://www.ofsted.gov.uk/provider/files/2012185/urn/107260.pdf/

Bibliography and further reading

Ofsted (2012c). *Inspecting E-Safety: Briefing for Inspectors*. Ref: 120196. Available at: http://www.ofsted.gov.uk/resources/briefings-and-information-for-use-during-inspections-of-maintained-schools-and-academies-september-2/

Ofsted (2012d). *Moving English Forward*. Ref: 110118. Available at: http://www.ofsted.gov.uk/resources/moving-english-forward/

Ofsted (2013). *School Inspection Handbook*. Ref: 120100. Available at: http://www.ofsted.gov.uk/resources/school-inspection-handbook/

Pang, Katherine (2009). 'Video-Driven Multimedia, Web-Based Training in the Corporate Sector: Pedagogical Equivalence and Component Effectiveness'. *International Review of Research in Open and Distance Learning* 10(3). Available at http://www.irrodl.org/index.php/irrodl/article/view/629/1265/

Parkin, Tony (2011). 'The Innovators: 25 David Mitchell'. Available at: http://agent4change.net/innovators/982-the-innovators-25-david-mitchell.html/

Pink, Daniel (2010). 'Think Tank: Flip-Thinking – The New Buzz Word Sweeping the US'. Available at: http://www.telegraph.co.uk/finance/businessclub/7996379/Daniel-Pinks-Think-Tank-Flip-thinking-the-new-buzz-word-sweeping-the-US.html/

Prensky, Marc (2001). 'Digital Natives, Digital Immigrants: Part 1', *On the Horizon* 9(5): 1–6. Available at: http://www.marcprensky.com/writing/prensky%20-%20digital%20natives,%20digital%20immigrants%20-%20part1.pdf/

Sams, Aaron (2011). 'There Is No Such Thing as THE Flipped Class'. Available at: http://chemicalsams.blogspot.co.uk/2011/10/there-is-no-such-thing-as-flipped-class.html/

Smith, Jim (2010). *The Lazy Teacher's Handbook: How Your Students Learn More When You Teach Less*. Carmarthen: Crown House Publishing.

Traxler, John (2009). 'Education and the Impact of Mobiles and Mobility: An Introduction to Mobiles in Our Societies'. Available at: http://www.academia.edu/205116/Education_and_the_Impact_of_Mobiles_and_Mobility/

Wheeler, Steve (2011). 'Misplaced ICT'. Available at: http://steve-wheeler.blogspot.co.uk/2011/05/misplaced-ict.html/

Bibliography and further reading

Wilshaw, Sir Michael (2012). 'The Importance of Teaching – Ofsted's View'. Speech delivered at the London Festival of Education, 17 November. Available at: http://www.ofsted.gov.uk/resources/importance-of-teaching-ofsteds-view-hmci-speech/

978-178135137-6

978-178135052-2

978-178135130-7